FINANCIAL
MANAGEMENT
for Clergy

A Guide to Personal and Family Finances

FINANCIAL MANAGEMENT
for Clergy

David L. Northcutt

Baker Book House

Grand Rapids, Michigan 49506

To

Conrad and Freda,
my parents

Bonham and Velma,
Bonnie's parents

Bonnie,
God's gift of love, my wife

Elizabeth and Christopher,
God's gift of joy, our children

Contents

Appendixes

Introduction

All ministers preach on the topic of stewardship at one time or another. Whether they talk about money, or responsibility, or spiritual devotion, what it comes down to is an accountability for the gifts which God has bestowed on us. Naturally, if we who are ministers are to practice what we preach, we are to be responsible for how we use what God entrusts to us. We cannot expect laymen to be responsible if we are not.

One of the most important things that God trusts to our care is our family. Thus, we must not only be "stewards of the mysteries of God," in the spiritual sense, but we must protect the material well-being of those who look to us for care and nurture. Toward that goal, this workbook can be used over and over again through the years.

To emphasize how important it is to consider the "material," even with a "spiritual" orientation, look at the parable of the talents. The positive statement of that parable is: To those who have, more will be given. Of course, it also makes the point that we are responsible for that which God gives us. To see how much God is entrusting to your stewardship, look at Appendix A. The table shows the annual salary of a young person who starts working for the church at age twenty, for $10,000 per year, and projects a 5 percent annual increase until age sixty-five. One column shows annual salary; the other column shows total cumulative salary at yearly intervals.

If your annual earnings are more than $10,000, use the ratio of your salary to $10,000 as a multiplier (example: salary of $25,000 yields multiplier of 2.5; salary of $30,000 yields multiplier of 3.0). Include not just your take-home pay but also the value of everything that is yours because you work for the church (free use of a house;

denominational life, hospitalization, and other insurance; contributions to pension plans; and so on). After determining your multiplier, go down the second column of the chart to the number of years until you expect to retire, say twenty-five years if you are now age forty. Move across to the fourth column of that line to total salaries to date ($477,315 for a $10,000 base). If your current salary is $35,000, multiply $477,315 by 3.5 and discover that with only a 5 percent increase each year, you will be entrusted with $1,670,602 by the time you are age sixty-five. The figure will be even higher if your increases are greater than 5 percent.

As a good steward, how will you handle all that material wealth during your lifetime? That is what this workbook is all about. It is a way for you to do some planning in the material areas of life so that once done, your financial management will require a minimum amount of time from then on. Since most ministers lack the time, skills, and inclination to do much complicated financial research, it is even more important to make the wisest use of what God entrusts to our care.

The information in this book is not a get-rich-quick scheme, nor a program to avoid paying bills that you already owe. Neither is it a magic formula for living like a king on a minimum wage. What this workbook will do is show you how to take charge of the financial areas of your life through the efficient use of your material assets, and how to reach your own long-term goals through the way you handle money in your day-to-day living.

We begin with a theological perspective, then move into the specifics of your financial planning. Remember, this workbook is of no use to you if you read it once, put it on the shelf, and never open it again. The worksheets take some time and may sound like too much effort, but the concepts are valid enough that you can modify the details of the nitty-gritty to suit your own theological and financial needs.

1

A Matter of Balance

Clergy may wrestle with a perplexing dilemma where personal finance is concerned. On the one hand they live in a world which requires money to buy food, clothes, shelter, piano lessons for children, and all the rest. Yet, at the same time, ministers are not supposed to worry about earthly treasures, but rather to seek the spiritual "kingdom of God." Many ministers feel guilty about desiring more money or even being concerned about what they receive. However, there is a responsible theological stance which says God gives us things in this world for our comfort, for which we are called to be responsible stewards, and therefore with which we must concern ourselves.

"To every thing there is a season," says Ecclesiastes. While Isaiah speaks of beating swords into plowshares and spears into pruning hooks, Joel talks about a time of strength, when plowshares are made into swords and pruning hooks into spears. For each circumstance there is a proper time and place. The apostle Paul realized that we often face apparently opposing ideas that have to be dealt with simultaneously. While he was indisputably concerned with the spiritual realm of life, Paul also dealt with the physical needs of orphans and widows by appointing deacons to look after their material welfare.

Solomon said to find wisdom by looking to the ant. Perhaps if he were alive today, he might advise looking to the inscription on a soft-drink bottle: "No Deposit/No Return." My parents used to say that "you get out of something according to what you put into it." Faced with the requirement that Christians have to be spiritual and yet live in the material world, Paul might also have agreed with the idea of "No Deposit/No Return" as a good way to keep a balance, to keep everything in perspective. In trying to handle the tension between spiritual and material realms, look to each and say, "No Deposit/No Return." If you exclude either by making no deposit, from that realm there will be no return.

Jesus told the parable of the rich fool who planned to build ever-bigger barns in which to store his material wealth—only to die in the midst of the planning. This was a warning not to neglect the spiritual while thinking of the material. But Jesus also told the parable of the talents and said to "render unto Caesar what is Caesar's." He had a disciple catch the fish with the coin in its mouth so that Caesar's tax could be paid for Jesus and all the apostles. We, too, are faced with the delicate balance between the spiritual and the material. We know that we cannot serve God and money equally and that we should not be "anxious about tomorrow." At the same time, we have responsibilities in the material world to feed, clothe, house, and care for those family members whom God has placed under our keeping. To fail to do so is to deny our faith in God.

The balance is kept by allotting the proper amount of time and concern to each area of life. "No deposit" in the spiritual will bring "no return" in the spiritual, and "no deposit" in the material means "no return" in that realm. Proper deposit, however, nets proper return in either area.

Money is a tangible symbol of material concerns and a medium of exchange for time and talent used in service of another. It is also a way to bypass bartering for goods and services. Without coins or bills, we would have to carry around such things as chickens, wood, or home-grown vegetables to trade for other items we desired. Money is a symbolic substitute for food items, tools, crafted products, skills, and artistry in the bartering process; it has no intrinsic value beyond its common acceptance in the trading system. United States currency formerly was backed by and/or made from gold or silver. Today we still use dimes and quarters, even though the coins are now made from something other than gold or silver, it is the symbolism that is important. Gold, silver, paper, or any other token of "money" has only the value that people assign in accepting it in trade for goods and services. (The word *salary* comes from the Latin for "salt," which was part of the pay of Roman soldiers, thus making it one of the earliest forms of money.)

You can calculate your material wealth in dollars, even if you have few of them (house equals $70,000; auto equals $6,000; and so on). You can place a dollar value on the work you do ($5.00 per hour, $15,000 per year, and so on). Since money has no value in itself, it is neither good nor bad, and is merely the symbol used to represent other aspects of life. "I spent X hours of my life earning that car or suit of clothes" is another way of saying that I spent $6,000 on that car or $70 on that suit.

The term *economics* comes from the Greek word for "house" or "housekeeping." If we wished to speak of "Christian economics," we might say it is the way a Christian keeps his or her house in order. Although the end result may often be the same as for a non-Christian, the motives are different. Whether Christian or non-Christian, one should care for one's family, but Paul's admonition is to do everything as a Christian witness. And Jesus instructs us to do what we do in the material world without displacing God as the ultimate object of worship. In other words, don't serve money instead of God, but rather use money to serve God.

There are so many texts in the Bible on money and the proper perspective toward the material world, that one can touch upon merely a few. For example, 1 Timothy 6:10 says that "the love of money is the root of all evil." Matthew 6:19–21 tells us that we should not store up treasures on earth. And Jesus warns in Matthew 25:14–30 that much will be required of those to whom much is given. When the early Christians believed that Jesus would return in their lifetime, they pooled their goods and held all things in common. They wished to be free of material concerns in order to concentrate on the spiritual. (Paul even advised against marriage, because one who is married has responsibilities which take one's mind off the purely spiritual.) All of that was very practical advice at the time. We would probably all live differently if we knew we were going to die within the week, month, or year. (While that is always a possibility, most people behave as if they expect to live indefinitely.) I know a family whose eleven-year-old child was dying of an illness that they knew would take the child within six months. That family lived differently during those months than they would have if they had expected the child to live to be sixty or seventy or eighty—a "normal" life-span.

Of course, Jesus did not return in their lifetime, and those early Christians had to adjust their thinking for the long haul. From that perspective, one must try to keep a spiritual orientation—for whether or not Jesus returns soon, we could go to Him at any time by being killed in a car wreck or becoming ill or dying suddenly overnight. However, we must also keep material things in perspective by caring for our families and ourselves as a witness to our faith. We must show our accountability to God by accepting responsibility for whomever (or whatever) God has entrusted to us: "But if any provide not for his own, and specially for his own house, he hath denied the faith, and is worse than an infidel" (1 Tim. 5:8).

Money—or the lack of it—is not as important as what we do with what we have. Job, Abraham, Solomon, and many other biblical figures were rich by the standards of their day (and perhaps by ours). Amos, several other prophets, and most early Christians were not rich. Yet, God used them all because they kept their proper perspective: proper deposits and returns in both the spiritual and material arenas of life. Responsibility without anxiety!

So how do we keep this proper balance? How do we know when we have made the proper deposits in both realms without being overly concerned with the material? It is sometimes difficult. Jesus decided to take whatever came—as we see when He said that although the foxes have holes and the birds have nests, He had nowhere to lay His head. Mohammed did not become a religious leader until after he had married a rich woman and could therefore spend his time on what he considered spiritual matters. Most of us are generally in between—neither rich nor willing to do completely without. I do not believe that God wants us to be totally destitute. So long as we keep a proper attitude about material things, we can serve God, yet also have "possessions."

Whatever we are doing in life should be a source of enrichment, accomplishment, and joy, not a cause for anxiety. If we are anxious about any of life's needs, we are not in balance. Remember, the value of money or any other material thing is related to what we do to attain it—and how we use it. I once read a story about a group of men who were hiking in the mountains. Since they had not planned to spend the night, they had not brought a lot of camping gear with them. A sudden snowstorm caught them by surprise. Because they were not well equipped, their only resources were what they had on their persons. They quickly gathered wood, but had no tinder with which to kindle the fire to keep warm and to signal for help. Then one of the men remembered that they all had paper money in their pockets. Hundreds of dollars in paper money were burned in order for them to survive!

Too often we only remember that money is merely a tool—not an end in itself—when we are forced to face this fact by the illness of a loved one or some other crisis in our lives. As good as were the tools of Stradivarius, we remember not the tools but the end product, his violins. If we use money or any material item to draw closer in our walk with God, keeping the spiritual and material in proper perspective, I believe He will bless what we do. No deposit, no return—proper deposit, proper return.

If you are reading this workbook, you are more than likely well trained to deal with your spiritual needs without my help. What I will try to do is help you to deal with the material side of life, so that you may thereby make the proper deposit.

"For unto whomsoever much is given, of him shall much be required . . ." (Luke 12:48).

2

Where Are You Now?

It is always a good idea to start at the beginning. If you were told you had to go to a certain place on earth and were given a map for guidance, you would first have to find your present location on the map. That is just what you need to do with your financial map: Find out where you are now. Later we will look at where you are going, but you will not know how far you have progressed along the road to that destination until you find your present position.

Look at Appendix B. Take time now to fill in the spaces on that table. Do not overlook anything. If you do not know something, find it out. For example, you need to know what it costs your church or employer to provide health insurance, because if you wanted the same coverage and no longer worked for that employer, it would cost you that much (or more) to get the same protection.

What you are worth financially is probably far more than you realized. Look not only at what you bring home in your paycheck, but also at all those extras that are paid for or reimbursed by your employer. Place a value on your furniture, automobile, clothing, dishes, everything you own that would cost you money to replace. Look in classified ads, go to garage sales, study a good mail-order catalog, and/or go to stores to see what similar items are selling for. Remember to allow for depreciation and the effects of inflation. While some of your possessions may not have much value in the current market, others may actually be worth more than you paid for them. Fill out Appendix B completely before proceeding to the next chapter.

3

Where Are You Going?

In *Alice in Wonderland,* Alice comes to a fork in the road and asks advice from the Cheshire Cat about which way she should go. The cat's answer is that the way she should go depends on where she wants to arrive. When Alice says she does not know her desired destination, the cat tells her that it then does not matter which way she goes. If you do not know which way you are going—what your ultimate goals and objectives are—you will not know how to make use of the rest of the information in this book.

Before going on, set aside some time to work through in your own mind the answers to three questions. (Your answers should cover the whole family if you are married, or at least take into account that your family will be going wherever you go.) Write down your answers in the book or on another sheet of paper. There is a quality about putting something in writing that makes you take it seriously.

1. What are all the things you value most in life? (For example, love of God, family, work, health, variety of experiences, security, service to others, and so on.)

2. When you reach the moment of death, if you were asked to look back over your life and mention what the accomplishments of that life had been, what would you like to be able to say?

3. In what way can your financial planning, your use of the money you will earn in your lifetime, help you accomplish your goals—and at the same time reflect your most valued ideas?

Now you will examine (and plan) your "lifeline." The assignment in Appendix C involves a vertical line which will represent the years of your life. The top number ("30" in our sample) indicates your present age. The figure at the bottom ("80") assumes that you will live that long—but you could extend the line even further if you wish to project your age past that number.

You will begin by preparing your lifeline—your road map to the future—by marking your present age on the line. This will be your starting point. Step One requires that you itemize on the line those events that have a high probability of occurring at certain ages. For an illustration, I have completed a chart for a hypothetical thirty-year-old minister with a wife (twenty-eight) and two children, aged three and five. It is most likely that each child will graduate from high school at age eighteen and go on to college or technical school. That would occur when their father is forty-three and forty-five. He will probably retire at sixty-five, so that fact is added to the line. A note is also made to the effect that this man expects his wife to outlive him and that some preparation should be made for this probability.

Illustrations for Step One and for the two steps that follow are shown in Appendix C.

Step Two consists of entering events that you would *like* to happen. Look at your answer to question two—things you would like to accomplish in life. Remember that just saying that you have these specific long-term goals gets nothing actually done! Pinpoint the times in your life when you would like to have accomplished each goal and mark those times on the line. (For example, at designated ages you might wish to be pastor of a certain-size congregation, earn a doctoral degree, serve on important denominational boards, travel around the world, and so on.)

In our illustration of Step Two, we assume that our young minister has been serving in a small church in a rural community and has mentioned goals of earning a doctorate; either teaching in seminary or pastoring in a large urban church; being able to aid his children in higher education and/or getting started in their own businesses; developing hobbies and other interests so that he will not be a dull person; traveling, especially after the children leave home; and having a comfortable retirement, including being able to leave his wife enough resources to live at a comfortable level after his death.

Our hypothetical subject picked the dates (his age) at which he would like to accomplish these things, and entered them on his lifeline. It is most important to choose specific ages for your goals—even if you miss meeting them by a few years or so. If you don't put goals down, you will probably not even work toward them. Your lifeline can always be revised to meet unexpected needs or changes in your aspirations. You cannot anticipate everything—a major illness which drains the family financially or the necessity for your aging parents to move in with you—but it is still better to have a plan than to be a ship without a rudder, sailing aimlessly through the years until one day you realize that you are about to retire and have accomplished little of value in your life.

Even if you are not exactly sure where you want to be eventually, including the career aims of your ministry, you can at least put down the goals of which you are reasonably certain, and then go on from there. Perhaps you do not know what career step you hope to achieve by age fifty, but between now and when you turn forty, you can explore various types of jobs within the church to determine possible options for the future. Even such an indefinite plan will steer you toward choices in line with your priorities.

In Step Three, you will go backward from the ages at which you hope to attain your goals and indicate when you will begin putting into action the activities which will help you toward each goal. Sample subgoals might be a saving-and-investment plan, acquiring certain skills, establishing a credit rating, and so on.

Many people daydream vaguely about doing something special in life, yet consider the ultimate goal(s) so unreachable that they keep putting off any action. If you break down your big idea into small manageable subgoals, and work on each one as it comes along, it is a lot easier to keep a hopeful eye on the ultimate prize. It also makes you see that *now* is the time to get started.

My favorite illustration of this point concerns a man who was unhappy with his job and where he was going (or not going) in life. One day he was talking to a friend and bemoaning the fact of his obligations to his wife and children, whereby he could not afford to go to college full-time and thus leave his dead-end job. If he went to college part-time at night, he would need ten years to earn a degree. His wise friend asked, "Where will you be in ten years if you *don't* go to college at night?" The man answered, "I guess I'll be doing just what I'm doing now." The friend persisted: "And what will you be doing if you go ahead and spend the ten years going to college at night?"

Making feeble excuses is a stalling technique which is often used to delay making decisions. You can always change your original plan, if at a later time you decide that God is leading you in a different direction, or if new opportunities open up for you unexpectedly. The main thing now is to have a plan for your life, instead of oozing along and drifting with the winds of the moment.

In the illustration for Step Three, the young man (who has already decided to earn a doctoral degree) does some advance planning by starting to make applications for a graduate program years before he actually begins his studies. After looking at his other priorities, he realizes that he must begin immediately to get his budget in shape so that he can meet not only his tuition, but expected expenses in all areas of his life plan. In the process, he can establish a good credit rating in anticipation of future borrowing needs, such as for his own and his children's education.

On the lifeline illustration of Step Three, are written the letters A, B, C, D, and E, with the corresponding plans of action added to the left of the line. Part of the immediate plan (A), for example, is to begin a systematic insurance program to guarantee that the goals for the family will be realized, even if the husband/father dies at an early age. The key is advance planning. Each of the items listed actually predates the hoped-for achievement by a number of years. For example, our friend wants to enjoy hobbies by age fifty-five. To that end, he will ask parishioners who are collectors, fishermen, wood-workers, and so on to teach him something about their hobbies (expecting that they will enjoy doing so).

Now it is your turn! Once you have finished plotting your lifeline on the form in Appendix C and begun to put into action the measures that will accomplish your goals and dreams, do not simply put this book aside and forget it! Use all the worksheets as directed, but at least once a year (perhaps around New Year's Day or during a vacation) sit down with your family and reevaluate your lifeline to see that it still reflects your priorities and goals. If so, reaffirm your broad plan, perhaps adding some other subgoals. If not, then change whatever no longer fits your aspirations.

This is not the sort of exercise to do during half-time of a TV football game. Set aside some time when your future is all you have to think about—and go through the questions again, readjusting your lifeline accordingly. As you grow, mature, and experience life more fully, attitudes and goals may change somewhat. You might also discover different approaches to the goals that are unchanged.

Although our sample refers to a young man of thirty, we should not assume that he is the only person completing this worksheet. He has a twenty-eight-year-old wife and two children. They should not feel that the lifeline is only *his,* for whatever happens to him affects their lives. The wife, for example, may wish to return to work full-time after the children leave home (or maybe before, if extra funds are needed for some of the goals). It may be possible (and necessary) to plan for such things as braces for the children's teeth by either saving money for that purpose or taking out dental insurance.

You and your family have individual needs and special circumstances, and your plan should be tailored to fit the family's life plan. This exercise can also be used as a training tool to help your children learn about taking responsibility for managing their own lives when they leave home.

When you have answered the questions at the beginning of this chapter and filled in the items on your lifeline (Appendix C), move on to the next chapter.

4

Money Management and Your Priorities

A wise man once said that he could tell you about your priorities in life if you allowed him a look at your checkbook or other records of your spending habits. What he meant was that most people tend to put their money where their hearts are. Accordingly, the first step is to manage your money so that it will reflect your goals, objectives, priorities—whatever you wish to call those items on your lifeline which you want to achieve.

Some things we do with our money are not really within our control. While we may shop around for the lowest prices, a significant amount of our money must be spent on food, clothing, and shelter, just to exist. We also have to pay for some form of transportation. There are unavoidable expenses for health care, for doctors, dentists, and medication. Obviously, the primary use of our money is for survival. There is also a price to pay for living in a civilized society—taxes to provide for education, protection, and law and order. While there are ways to cut costs for basic needs (and even ways to pay as few taxes as possible), we cannot eliminate these expenses entirely.

Once we have provided for the basic survival of ourselves and our families, we can move into the areas which make life comfortable, meaningful, and enjoyable. Even survival expenditures can reflect your goals and values in life. For example, by spending more on a well-balanced diet, you show that you value good physical health. By eating at fast-food establishments, you may indicate that you would rather spend your time in other ways than cooking and dining leisurely. If you drive a ten-year-old car, you reveal certain values (and by driving a new sports car, you do, too). But beyond the subsistence level of the budget, how you spend (or don't spend) and/or invest and save your money greatly reflects your basic values and determines how fast you will reach the goals you wish to achieve in your lifetime.

There are no recommended percentages to spend on food, clothing, and shelter which could apply to everyone. According to statistics, the more money one makes, the less will be the percentage spent on the survival areas and the more spent in such categories as entertainment or savings. To begin to manage your money in a way which reflects your goals, you must be realistic. If you are now using all your money on absolute necessities, and just barely staying above debt, it would be unrealistic to think you could buy that camping trailer tomorrow, since you obviously have no room in the budget for "extras."

Examine Your Spending Habits

Begin where you are right now. Sit down with your checkbook and other financial records and compute what you spent in the last twelve months for the areas listed in Table 1 at the end of this chapter (Page 00). I will explain each item in detail as we go along. You may wish to read the rest of this chapter before you go through your records—just so you will know what to enter where. But, whether or not you do so, calculate what you have spent during the past year for each category before moving on to the next step, which will be explained later.

Entering your annual expenditures in each category will probably take some careful digging into your records! Your task will be simpler if you habitually log all your expenses as they occur. Most people are not that meticulous, however, and may have to supplement their records with their memory or even some educated guesswork. If that describes your current record keeping (or lack of it), you will quickly learn to be more precise in the future.

1. Church/Charities. Although this is not actually a basic survival category, I have listed it first for an important reason. In my value system, God plays a very important role, as do charities. By placing this first on my listing, I am saying that this is a reflection of all the other values in my life.

2. Savings/Investments. See chapter 8 for a full explanation of this item.

3. Food/Household Items. Ideally, we should divide this into two separate categories, but most people do not have time to go through each grocery ticket and differentiate food from nonfood items, so I have listed them together. This category will include food and anything needed to run the house (cleaning supplies, paper products, and so on). If you shop at one of the supermarket giants that sell clothes, plumbing equipment, and everything for an automobile, try to earmark items for which there is a separate listing on the budget worksheet. Include eating-out expenses when this is just "for convenience." When you eat out to celebrate (birthdays, anniversaries, parties), use that specific category.

4. Clothing. This is where you may have to do some research to make sure that you assign all the expenditures into the proper category. If you charge things at a department store or on a major credit card, itemize amounts spent for clothing and for the other categories on the list. If you let the credit card bill go long enough to accumulate interest and service charges, add those to the cost of the clothing (or the other items) if it is easy to figure; if not, put interest and service charges under the Miscellaneous category.

5. Shelter. This listing includes three different subheadings.

Mortgage/Rent represents the basic cost of a roof over your head, either rent or—if you are buying a home—principal and interest payments on the mortgage, insurance on the house and its contents, property taxes on the house and land. In short, enter here all costs to own the property, even if you did not actually live there. If the church furnishes you with a house, enter the fair rental value here.

Utilities are sometimes covered partially or totally in rent payments. If such is your case and you do not know the exact cost of the utilities, just lump them all together at this point. If you (or the church) pay them yourself, list everything provided by private or public companies (water, sewer charges, garbage collection, electricity, gas, telephone, cable television, and so on). If you subscribe to cable television, the basic rate should be listed under utilities, but any extras such as a movie channel or burglar and medical alarms should be listed under the categories they best fit, such as Entertainment or Medical.

Furniture/Miscellaneous speaks for itself. Anything related to the house and property that is not already accounted for goes in this slot, including repairs and normal maintenance.

6. **Transportation.** These costs may vary according to where you live and how you get around. If you own a car, the items to be listed under transportation are obvious. *Miscellaneous* is a convenient catchall. It can include parking fees, toll fees, bus, subway, and/or taxi charges, or anything else that relates to getting you places for which you have to pay, including payments to someone with whom you car-pool. Since it is hard to separate business and nonbusiness expenses for a pastor's car, include them both.

7. **Medical.** This category includes everything to do with health care—physician, dentist, ophthalmologist, eyeglasses, medication, and special equipment and appliances required for health. (Exercise equipment prescribed by a doctor would go here, but the same equipment purchased just because you like to exercise would go under Rest/Relaxation.)

8. **Personal Taxes.** Here you enter income and taxes other than those paid on your home, car, investments, and so on. If your state has a sales tax or value-added tax and it is not too hard to figure, it could go here, but it is probably easier just to include these as part of the cost of clothing or whatever the value addition was for.

9. **Insurance.** List here expenses for all insurance relating to people: life, health, accident, disability, or whatever. Insurance on your house, automobile, and other property is an expense which comes with owning these items, so such insurance premiums go under their respective categories. If you have borrowed against the cash value of life insurance, include the interest on those loans in this category. Be sure to count any insurance paid for by your employer (partially or in full). Even if it is not in your take-home pay, you have earned this benefit, and if you leave your current church, you will either have to find another employer to provide this coverage, or pay for it yourself.

10. **Allowances/Personal Care.** This is almost a miscellaneous category, but it really needs to be as separate an item as possible. Haircuts and beauty shop bills are personal-care items. (You may wish to place the cost of a health-club membership here rather than under the Rest/Relaxation category.) Everyone in the family should have an allowance which they may "blow" in any way they wish without having to be accountable to the total budget (even if it is

only the price of a soft drink). Children can be taught about budgets through the use of their allowances ("If the quarter is not spent this week on a soft drink, next week you will have enough to buy a fifty-cent toy"). If children wish to buy their own clothes in greater quantities than the family clothing budget allows, use of their allowance in that area is fine. Adults also need to have such no-strings-attached money. Be careful, however, not to allow use of this area as a way to tease other members of the family ("I used *my* allowance to buy you a present and you just spent *yours* on yourself"). Parents ought to provide guidance, and should not permit children to do just *anything* with their allowances, but so long as they are spending for a morally acceptable purpose, allowances should be personal, for both children and adults.

11. Entertainment. We all entertain ourselves and others to some extent—from chips and dips with the young-adult class to taking friends out to eat on their anniversary. This expense includes money spent on movies, plays, concerts, sports events. If you have a cable TV hookup, include here the cost of the *extra* entertainment features such as Home Box Office, Showtime, and the other movie, sports, and entertainment channels, partly because you will be spending the time at home instead of going out to be entertained for an admission fee.

12. Celebrations. Joyous special occasions are a part of the lives of most people. They take various forms from one family to another, but they fulfill a necessary function. Thus, celebrations ought to be included in our budget process, so that they are given appropriate consideration. That does not mean we have to spend a lot of money on them, just that they are taken into account. Birthdays, anniversaries, or other memorable events in the life of individuals and the family as a whole merit an appropriate celebration. Christmas is also included in this category, as are other religious or secular holidays.

13. Rest/Relaxation. It is impossible to work all the time without paying for it in physical, mental, or other symptoms. Everyone needs time off for rest and relaxation. Again, this category does not require a lot of money in the budget, but it should be taken into account as a reflection of what we are doing with our lives. Include here vacation expenses, costs of pursuing a hobby such as photography or stamp collecting, and general expenditures for your recreational needs.

14. Education/Enrichment. If we are to broaden our lives, we should not stop learning after we finish our formal education. We need to learn until we die. This category covers art and music lessons, books, magazines, book clubs, or any other educational endeavors that widen your experience beyond your normal work and hobbies.

15. **Professional Expenses.** Any educational requirements to improve the way you perform your ministry are listed in this category—as are tools, books, travel, or anything else needed to carry out your job (but not covered by your employer). If you receive educational or other profession-related allowances, include only what you spend from your personal budget over what the allowances provide.

16. **Community Involvement.** If you give to charities, such as United Way or Boy or Girl Scouts, in the form of money, that is listed under Charities. But if you participate in something like scouting to the extent that you are buying uniforms, taking trips, and so on, that is a matter of Community Involvement. This commitment may take the form of work for a political party, or membership in a chamber of commerce or Lions International.

17. **Prior Debt Retirement.** If you have planned your life in such a way that you wish to accomplish certain things in the future, you must save and budget for them accordingly. But if you already have debts from former expenditures, you have to fulfill those obligations as well. Later debts contracted for will be placed in the relevant categories as they are paid off—but prior debt repayment has a category all its own. (As soon as that debt is repaid, this category is dropped.)

18. **Miscellaneous.** Have we covered everything? Probably not. Even though there is a category in your budget for almost everything you will meet as you go through life, there always appears an unexpected something that we do not know where to place in the budget. The Miscellaneous category is reserved for that every-few-years or once-in-a-lifetime happening. The first time I planned a budget, this category was allotted almost 50 percent of the money. There is always the temptation to do that because it is easier than deciding in which category an expenditure goes. Try not to fall into that pattern; use the Miscellaneous listing as sparingly as possible.

19. **Totals.** The total spent last year should equal all that you received as income. This is the one time that "miscellaneous" may represent a larger amount than other times, just to balance these two totals.

Once you have entered your yearly totals for each category, determine the percentage of your total income which was spent for each major grouping. Do this by dividing each subtotal by your total income. List these figures in the second column of the annual budget.

Budget for Your Dreams

Your next budget concern involves a look into the future. If you are sincere about meeting your life's goals, accenting your value systems, and making your dreams come true, you will have to plan your budget carefully. At the end of each year—from now on—you should analyze the expenditures of the prior twelve months. Then you must ask yourself how you want your income spent in the next twelve months. Perhaps you want to change the percentages in column two—a larger share for contributions, more savings, or perhaps a lesser share for your investment program?

Be realistic! If your habit was to spend freely on entertainment or a hobby, or you were generous with lavish gifts to your children, it may be difficult to change your ways overnight, especially if a large debt must be repaid in the coming year. Whatever the situation, you must be practical and face reality. Drastic budget shifts may be impossible. Perhaps a better approach would involve revision in some category by only a percentage point or two. However, you must decide which budget categories you want to raise or lower—reflecting, of course, your ultimate goals, values, and dreams.

A five-year plan may be the answer to your goal of a stated percentage in each category of your budget. Raising the actual budgeted amount in some areas by one-fifth per year may be the most realistic means of attaining the goals you have set. (You will have to lower some figures to offset the increases in others.) If, after thorough analysis, you come to the conclusion that your last budget was already "tight," you may decide that any major change would be upsetting. In that case, commit yourself to the retirement of outstanding debts. Once these are taken care of, you may have the opportunity to increase spending elsewhere.

After you have written down the adjusted percentages, figure the amount of money for each category by reversing the way you calculated the original percentages. This time, multiply the percentages by total annual income to determine the money budgeted for each category, for example:

$$\$10,000 \times .20 \ (20\%) = \$2,000$$
$$\$10,000 \times .02 \ (\ 2\%) = \$ \ \ 200$$

Appendix D-1 is a monthly budget worksheet for which an imaginary completed form is also provided. In the first column, enter the amounts you have just determined as your adjusted budget for this year. Then divide each figure by twelve and enter it in the second column as your monthly allotment (the amount you can spend monthly on this item in order to attain the desired accomplishments on your lifeline). The temptation will be to keep on spending as before, and it may be hard at first to cut down, especially in those areas where you must also make a cut to balance the increase in another category. But, each month, if you will look at your life plan and at your answers to the questions in chapter 3, your motivation for these economies will be reinforced. As you realize success in the areas where your expenditures reflect what you most value, selective cuts will become a way of attaining your goals and dreams.

Of course, someone might say, "This is a lot of work, and if I were disciplined about records in the first place, I wouldn't need to do all this." That may be true to some extent, but not entirely. In the first place, many people float through life without a plan. Even though they may be able to keep records of how money was spent, the way it was spent did not really get them closer to an ultimate goal or reflect their conscious values. The point of this workbook is not just to give you a place to keep records but to help you see how spending your money gets results, in that it shows yourself, your family, and the world your values and goals in life. If you can do that *without* record keeping, you are an exceptional person. For most people, records are a necessary bother. They help you see if you are within your self-imposed limits so that you may find ways to spend more in the areas that have more meaning to you.

At the end of each month, add up the amount spent in each category and then enter it in the Spent This Month column. Then, just to see how you are doing for the year, add that amount to the Spent This Year column from the previous month. Enter this new total on the current month's page. (It may help your own completion of this worksheet if you take a look at the sample provided for our imaginary family in Appendix D.)

As an additional tool, there is also a page for listing bills to be paid each month. (See Appendix D-2.) Such a record indicates checks

Table 1

Annual Budget Worksheet
19_____

Budget Category	Spent Last Year	Percent of the Total Budget	New Percent to Reflect Life Values/ Goals	Adjusted Budget for This Year
Church/Charities				
Savings/Investments				
Food/Household Items				
Clothing				
Housing: Mortgage/Rent				
Utilities				
Furniture/Miscellaneous				
Transportation: Auto Payments				
Gas, Oil, Etc.				
Insurance				
Repairs/Maintenance				
Miscellaneous				
Medical (doctor, dentist, medicine)				
Personal Taxes (income/other)				
Insurance (life, health, other)				
Allowances/Personal Care				
Entertainment (at home and away)				
Celebrations (holidays, birthdays, anniversaries, etc.)				
Rest/Relaxation (vacations, hobbies, recreation, etc.)				
Education/Enrichment (art/music lessons, books, etc.				
Professional Expenses (tools, books, schools, not paid by employer)				
Community Involvement (political parties, scouting, etc.)				
Prior Debt Retirement				
Miscellaneous				
TOTALS				

which must be drawn each month to credit-card companies and other payees. Remember that portions of some of these check amounts must be allocated to the proper category on the monthly budget worksheet. The sample will indicate how the figures are assigned to such categories as gasoline, clothes, medicine, and so on.

At the end of the book there are enough blank forms for each worksheet to take you through a year of budget planning.

Since some of the items deserve more in-depth discussion, the chapters immediately following will expand on the basic principles of allocating your money so that it works for you.

5

Insurance for Now—and Later

If you make plans to live to age seventy, eighty, or ninety, or even a hundred, and set goals to live with until then—and *if* you stay healthy and work and die according to your plan—and *if* your home does not burn, and your car is not wrecked, and no thief breaks in to steal—then all is well. That's a lot of *if's!* However, houses do burn, autos are wrecked, and people do die "too young" or become disabled. The way to be assured that such disasters do not upset your life plan is to take out insurance—both people insurance (life, health, and disability) and property insurance. There is a place for such protection in everyone's financial planning, and the goals on your lifeline should determine how much and what types of insurance to have.

The philosophy of property/casualty insurance is simple. If there are 10,000 houses in a town and each year one house is totally destroyed by fire and each house costs $10,000, the townspeople could protect themselves by having each homeowner put one dollar per year into a fund for the one homeowner who will lose his or her house that year. A small fee would be added to cover administrative costs and profit for the underwriting company, but that is the philosophy on which insurance is based. You may think that you are paying in advance for your possible future problems (which you hope never to have) but what is really being done is that those paying each year are covering the problems of those who will have losses—plus administrative costs and profit margins for the insurance company who provides the service. If the company holding the policies has to pay an unusually large amount in fire insurance claims one year, everyone will probably have to pay higher premiums the

35

following year, to make up the difference. Whether you rent your living quarters or own them, it is essential to take out insurance against damage or theft of your property, as well as liability protection against claims by those who may be injured or have property damaged while on your premises.

Life insurance assumes basically the same philosophy, but rates are based on figures which project the number of people of a given age who are expected to die each year. (See Appendix E for a typical Mortality Table.) The statistics also estimate the number in a given age group who will still be living at the end of the year. Because of differences in life expectancy, if you start buying life insurance when you are relatively young, it will cost you less per year than it would for an older person.

This possible oversimplified explanation depicts the way insurance works (with slight variations). Although the insurance company is entitled to a profit for its service, you should shop around to find the most protection for your money, as well as the coverage which best fits your needs. Insurance provides a measure of security and stability for you and your family, and you need an amount in proportion to your responsibilities, property worth, and goals. There are different types of insurance to cover your particular situation, need, and ability to pay. Your goals and values will tell you something about how much insurance is enough. Since you cannot possibly insure against everything, first insure against the most probable disaster. Later, as you can afford more, get other coverage to broaden your protection and security. Look at your lifeline to decide what you should protect. It will then be easier for the agent to help you. It is unwise to let an agent sell you a policy just to insure a limited need such as a mortgage or your children's education, rather than trying to protect your total life plan. The brokerage firm which handles my money-market fund advises that before anyone starts investing in such things as stocks (which is how a broker makes money), he or she should have first made sure that all insurance is in proper shape. Insurance varies so much from state to state and company to company that I will limit my discussion to the two basic types of life insurance.

Term insurance is for temporary needs. You can get it at banks to cover your loans, as well as from insurance agents. For the life of the policy, you pay a fee based on your age when you begin. (Such a policy on an auto loan would be just for the term of the loan.) Term life is a good way to cover—for the least amount of money—a time in your life when you have high responsibilities (children to educate, for example). The term can be for a few years or many, but as you get older, either the premiums go up or the protection goes down, as we shall explain later.

Permanent life insurance is usually purchased for the period of time from your present age to age 100 or death, whichever comes first, and the premiums are fixed at a set amount for the total years of the policy. The younger you start, the lower the premiums (for example, a $10,000 policy for a man of twenty-five might cost him $150 per year until age 100, but the same policy for a man of thirty-five would be over $200 per year). In theory, the younger man would pay premiums until age 100, when he would receive $10,000 back from the company. Since the thirty-five-year-old man has ten fewer years to pay in enough to cover $10,000, he must pay higher premiums. Of course, if either dies before his hundredth birthday, the survivors receive $10,000 regardless of how much has been paid.

A variation of this policy charges higher premiums but pays the $10,000 at age sixty-five. (This is called an endowment policy.) Another type has the insured pay a slightly higher premium until age sixty-five—or some other age—then make no other payment for the rest of his life. (This is a paid-up policy.) These permanent policies are really term insurance (the term is to age 100 or death) on which the higher premiums paid later in life are averaged with the lower early premiums. Since one pays slightly more than for normal term when younger, but *much* less than for normal term in later life, this is often called whole-life insurance.

Features and Benefits of the Base Policy

"Benefits" are what you or your beneficiary receive from an insurance policy. "Features" are the details of the policy that provide these benefits.

In a life-insurance policy, the primary benefit is that—for the amount of your annual premiums—you gain peace of mind in the knowledge that no matter what happens to you, the goals and dreams that money can provide (a home, education for children, monthly income for survivors) will be available for your family. There are many features which make all that possible. Some are part of the base policy; others are added on as riders.

One important basic feature is that your policy be *guaranteed renewable* and *noncancellable.* This means that once you have the policy, so long as you make your premium payments on time, the company cannot take it away from you for any reason other than fraud.

With regard to the corporate structure of the insurance company, there are two kinds of policies, *par* and *non-par (participating* and *non-participating).* If an insurance company does well on its investments, keeps overhead low, and does not have a large number of claims above the normal, there is money left over to distribute to its stockholders and/or policyholders. If it has stockholders all the money may go to them, or it may be split between the stockholders and policyholders. Since a mutual company has no stockholders, distributions go to the policyholders. This return is called a dividend. Legally, an insurance dividend paid to a policyholder is considered a refund of premiums, so it is not taxable as are stock dividends. If your insurance policy pays dividends, it is a participating (or par) policy; if not, it is non-participating (or non-par).

There is a fairly widespread philosophy that it is better to purchase term insurance and invest the difference saved by not paying the higher premiums on a permanent-type policy. Appendix F-1 to F-5 contains charts for ages twenty-five, thirty, thirty-five, forty, and forty-five which show how much you must make on investments to have more money value at age sixty-five than you would have in a cash-value/whole-life policy for which dividends were used to purchase paid-up additions. The net gain (after deducting expenses, taxes, losses, brokers' fees) must be *over* 8 percent if you are in a 25 percent tax bracket, 10 percent in a 40 percent tax bracket, or 12 percent if you are in a 50 percent tax bracket. That allows for only federal income tax. If your state has its own income tax, your gain must be even more.

The easiest way to accumulate cash while providing insurance protection is with a cash-value/whole-life policy, especially if you are limited in resources and time to devote to studying the stock market and/or managing an investment such as rental property. Using dividends to buy paid-up additions produces no hassle, no management problems, no fear for business loss. After deciding how much you can spend on insurance and investments, look again at your lifeline. If spending a lot of time looking after investments fits your goals, you may very well be able to make more than the percentages needed to exceed the cash value of a permanent policy. If you wish to try, however, get a good term policy first. After five or ten years (write that down on your lifeline so you won't forget to check), see if your investments are doing as well as you hoped. If so, great; if not, shift to a permanent policy and forget the hassle.

Please note that the term and whole-life policies used as illustrations in this workbook are not for comparison with policies you might have, but for drawing conclusions about buying term and investing the savings in contrast to buying whole-life. The illustrations represent sound, reasonably priced term and whole-life policies which have moderate to conservative dividend projections. There are term policies that are very much less expensive if you stay healthy, and whole-life policies that will pay great dividends and produce very high cash values and death benefits if their dividends can be paid at today's high rate for twenty to forty years. Rather than use such extremes, I prefer the more conservative approach. The charts can give you a feel for the kind of investment return needed if you are to equal or beat the whole-life policy. If you enjoy working with investments and/or do extremely well at investing, buying term and investing the difference might fit your style—even if you could find a whole-life policy that does much better than our illustrations. Some companies are making projections that show the twenty-five-year-old as attaining a cash value of between $300,000 and $400,000 by age sixty-five, for example. There will always be someone who can show you a "better" investment or insurance policy. Base your decisions on your goals and lifeline, not on "maybe" and "if."

Features Available as Riders

1. *Waiver of Premium* obligates the company to continue paying insurance premiums for you if you become totally disabled. That means that even if you cannot earn a living because of disability, you will not lose your insurance protection. This feature usually is extremely inexpensive.

2. *Accidental Death Benefit* usually pays an additional amount in the event of accidental death. Since this can be as high as the face value of the base policy, some people call it double indemnity, although it

could be more or less than double. Because most people do not die from accidents, I would rather see them purchase more face value on the base policy than a smaller base policy with an added ADB rider. Buy enough coverage to fulfill your dreams for your family, even if you "die too soon." Although it is 100 percent certain that you will die, the odds are against your meeting an accidental death.

3. *Option to Purchase* is a feature that guarantees the insured the right to purchase certain amounts of additional insurance at some time in the future (such as birthdays, marriage, birth or adoption of children)—even if the insured has become uninsurable (for example, after a heart attack). In a sense, this is insurance to be able to purchase insurance. Just like any insurance, if you need it, you *really* need it, so I highly recommend it.

4. *Term Insurance Rider* may be added to a permanent policy. The two basic term policies are level term (death benefit remains level) or *decreasing* or *reducing term* (death benefit reduces each year). The latter is often called mortgage protection, because the rate of decrease usually corresponds with the rate of a mortgage reduction. With level term, the premiums go up each year or on a "step rate" every five or ten years. With decreasing term, the premium remains level.

5. *Convertibility* is a feature to look for on term insurance, whether as a rider of a separate policy. This means that you may change at some point in the future to a permanent policy without proof of insurability. If you have an illness or a heart attack without this feature, you either must continue to pay increasing rates year after year, or face the problem of having no insurance when your decreasing term reduces to zero. If there is a convertibility clause, you can convert to a permanent policy, paying the slightly higher premiums at the time—but freezing the death benefit and premiums at a level rate for life.

Variations

While there are only two basic types of life insurance, permanent and term, there are many variations and combinations with a multitude of names.

Adjustable Life is a policy that is a combination of permanent and term. After telling the agent how much you want to pay and how much coverage you want, the policy automatically adjusts between permanent and term coverage to give you what you want. There are minimums—you cannot get $1,000,000 coverage for one dollar per year!

Universal Life combines term-type insurance with an investment factor, so the cash value may eventually be much much greater than it would be in a permanent life insurance policy. However, at the time of this writing, there were some tax questions that not been resolved about the investment portion of universal life.

Deposit Term is really a step-rate term policy, usually on a ten-year cycle. A policyholder pays a deposit, usually a double premium for the first year, and then regular level premiums for ten years. At the end of the ten years, he or she gets back all or most of the premium payments and can then start the whole process over with another large deposit and higher premiums for the next ten years. If the policy is dropped before a ten-year cycle is over, nothing is returned. This type of policy is usually sold along with an annuity (See chapter 11 on retirement for a detailed discussion.) The selling point is usually that this produces higher cash values than permanent insurance, while giving the protection of term. The above may be true with the permanent policies of some companies but not all. Almost any company's term and annuity can produce the same results. If you are told by an agent that you need to give up your current permanent policies to purchase a deposit-term-plus-annuity plan, at least give your present company's agent the chance to show you what he has that can do the same job. A sound permanent policy with a dividend option to purchase paid-up insurance can have a high cash value and also provide your beneficiary, after only a few years, with not only the original face value of the policy, but enough extra to equal or surpass the premiums paid. (See Appendix F-1 to F-5.)

How Much Life Insurance Do I Need?

There are rule-of-thumb answers to that question which range anywhere from six times annual salary to ten times annual salary, but that is a totally impersonal way to look at needs that are unique to each individual. A single person who does not plan to marry (and for whom there is no possibility of being responsible for aging parents or other family members) needs to have a totally different insurance program from the married man or woman who has several children and a mortgaged home, who wants to help the children through medical school, and provide for a spouse in the event of death. It also matters how much one already has in the way of investments (or lack thereof). A man about to retire who owns his own home and has no children living at home does not need the same protection as a young man with responsibilities just arising. Neither does the older man need as much if he has saved and invested through the years and now has a large annuity, holdings in real estate and stocks, and an expected inheritance from his aged mother who is about to die and leave him the family farm—with oil leases! In short, you need to work out your own unique needs and not base your calculations on some catchall formula that does not allow for your dreams.

First, look at your lifeline and the things you want to accomplish in life. Try to put a dollar value on those things that money can buy, such as college education for the children, piano and soccer lessons and summer camp, and a debt-free home for your spouse. Decide how much you would like the family to live on if you were not around. Deduct whatever you normally consume from the family budget (food, clothing, use of transportation, and so on). As an adult, you probably use slightly more than an equal share—and if there are two adults and two children in your family, you may use about 30 percent or so of the outlay, under normal circumstances. You should have two sets of figures: the total of the lump sums needed for such things as paying off the mortgage (which a surviving spouse may decide not to do, but for which the money should be available anyway), educating the children, and so on—plus the desired annual income for your family to live on. Studies have shown that it is wise to add about one year's salary (more or less) to the lump-sum total, just to cover such final expenses as the funeral, as well as emergencies that could not be handled easily by the daily living allowance. For example, while you are alive, if the family car were to die, you could probably borrow enough to buy a used or new replacement, but it might not be so easy for a surviving family member to do so.

To find the amount of insurance needed to provide what you would like your surviving spouse (or other beneficiary) to have, look at Appendix G. This section shows how long a given amount of annual income can be provided by $100,000 of capital under varying plans of investment and withdrawal. If you wish to assume inflation rates of about 10 percent, and want your survivor to have a specified amount of money each year until the money runs out (adjusted for inflation), look at the items in Figure G-1. If you want the survivor to be able to withdraw only an equal annual amount for a specified length of time, look at Figure G-3, which shows for given interest rates how much can be withdrawn each year to totally deplete $100,000 in five through thirty years.

The best way to look at things, in my opinion, is to invest the capital and use only a portion of the income each year, putting some back into the pot all the time. The capital pool then gets larger, producing a greater income each year, so that inflation is taken care of in the daily living area. A sample of this approach is shown in Figure G-3. If you want your spouse and/or survivors to live on twice or three times a certain annual income for X number of years, just assume you need a base that many times $100,000.

Now add that base amount to the lump sum you had allocated for college education, mortgage payoff, and so on. That is the total capital your family will need to replace your economic worth to the family. Since you probably already have some assets that could be used as capital (stocks, real estate), you now deduct their value from the amount of money needed to produce what you need to provide for your family if you are not here. The difference represents how much insurance you need. What astounds most people is that this figure is usually much larger than the insurance they now carry.

If you do not carry the recommended amount of insurance, the things you have put on the lifeline as important to you and your family will have no chance of being fulfilled. Before you start any kind of investment program to meet other parts of your life goals, you should first make sure that you have enough insurance to cover those goals and dreams. Start with a permanent-policy base and add term to make up the difference. If you cannot do that and stay within your budget, get all term insurance.

Term or Permanent Insurance?

Term insurance has the great advantage of being relatively inexpensive. At any age, it is cheaper than starting a permanent policy at the same age. The disadvantage is that if you are going to purchase a policy today and keep it until you die (even if you are eighty when you die), it will cost you much more than a permanent policy over the years. The reason is that a term policy goes up in cost per $1,000 of protection with each passing year. A permanent policy begins much higher in premiums than the term, but its premiums never increase, and if you receive dividends, by age sixty-five the dividends are often more than the premiums.

One advantage to whole life is that you can borrow from the policy. As premium payments are made, the policy accumulates a cash value and loans may be obtained from the insurance company up to that amount. The cash value never equals the amount of the premiums paid unless the policy pays dividends and you do something with the dividends to build up your cash value. (The insurance company must take out some for administrative costs and profit). The good thing about this feature is that money borrowed from a whole-life policy usually requires payment of interest which is substantially lower than what you would pay at a bank. If you borrow from the policy and die before repaying the amount borrowed, the insurance company deducts the amount of the loan from what they would pay your beneficiaries.

The biggest questions you really have to answer are whether you want insurance that goes up in price each year or want to pay a fixed amount for as long as you live—and whether the cash-value feature of whole-life is important for your needs.

Health and Disability Insurance

After life insurance has been acquired in adequate amounts to protect your goals for your family, you should also look at the area of health (insurance for hospitalization and disability). Many churches provide hospitalization for pastors and their families. Sometimes the denomination merely makes it available, and the pastor must pay for it himself, or perhaps pay for family coverage. Some policies cover only major medical expenses; others cover everything from eyeglasses to dental work. Get the best value you can for the money, in line with your overall goals and values. It is possible to have so much insurance that most of your money is spent on what *might* happen, rather than on making other things materialize.

Another policy to consider is disability insurance. Do not confuse this with accident insurance. A good disability policy will cover being disabled from accidents and also provide income in case of disability caused by an extended illness such as a heart attack. If you shop around, you can find good disability coverage for almost the same premium as accident insurance—and have a lot more for your money.

When looking for disability protection, the idea is to replace income lost when unable to work. When you are relatively young, the odds are greater that you will have a long-term disability of ninety days or more before age sixty-five than that you will die before that age. A long-term inability to earn income can hurt your goal-achievement by as much as or more than death. At least if you died while adequately insured, there would be money for your family's needs.

Things to look for in a disability policy are (1) definition of disability; (2) noncancellability; (3) definition of when the disabling condition is known; (4) standard exclusions; and (5) coverage for *both* sickness and accident.

Probably the most important feature of such a policy is the definition of disability. A large majority of policies specify *total* disability, not just inability to do something at full capacity. Get a policy that has a liberal definition of disability. Such coverage will cost more than a policy which stipulates total disability, but it is better to spend a few or even a hundred dollars a year more for something of value than to spend the money on a product that will not meet your needs when you have to use it.

Next in importance are the noncancellable and guaranteed-renewable features. It is no good to have a policy that is cancelled or not renewed by the company after you use it once. Features that guarantee that you can renew—and which the company cannot cancel as long as you pay your premiums—do not really cost anything substantial. Either the policy has these features or it does not. If it does not, don't get the policy!

A most important clause is the one which defines when the existence of a disabling condition is established. Your policy should clearly state that the disability is not established until *you* are aware of it. Otherwise, you might lose potential benefits, for example, if your doctor and/or spouse knew about your illness (but you did not) before the effective date of the policy.

Many policies have standard exclusions such as war, riot, and pregnancy. The very best policies have no exclusions except those which stipulate that pregnancy is not covered for a "reasonable period" such as ninety days (to keep someone from deciding a week before childbirth to take out the policy).

Example

A man goes to his doctor and has several tests done. The next day he goes to the insurance agent, fills out the application for disability insurance, and truthfully says that at the time he does not know of any medical problems. The policy is issued. Then the doctor calls the man in and tells him he has cancer. With treatments the man functions well for several years, but then the cancer gets to the point the man can no longer work and is thus disabled.

With some insurance contracts, even though the man said on the application that he truthfully knew of no problems, the doctor knew. Thus, even though the disability did not happen for years, the condition which led to the disability was discovered before the policy went into effect, so some companies would not pay.

The best contracts state that the person who is insured must know of the disability-causing problem before the contract is issued or the company will pay. Thus, in the above example, even though the doctor knew, the man did not, so the company will pay.

There are many more disabilities due to illness than to accidents. Thus a policy that covers only accident disability is much cheaper, but also much less likely to be used. Since you are dealing with your life's goals and dreams, don't be "penny wise and pound foolish." Get the policy that covers both sickness and accidents.

If you are buying a house or a car, you are probably required by the lender to carry insurance, so I will not go into detail on those types of policies. The only thing to check here is that you can get full-replacement-value coverage for a reasonable amount. On my own policy which covers both my house and its contents, I got full-replacement coverage for items stolen or lost or damaged in fire—for only 10 percent more. With the cost of everything from dishes to sofas going ever higher, I felt this was a reasonable extra to buy. (A tip from a photographer friend: photograph each room of your house taking four pictures per room, standing with your back against each wall. Put those pictures in your safe deposit box. If your house is destroyed by fire or you have a burglary, you will have a way to show the insurance company what you had. It is also advisable to keep a complete inventory of your possessions.)

Speaking of safe deposit boxes, I should point out that in case of death some states may not let the survivors take items from the box right away. To avoid delay in life-insurance claims, do not put your policies in your safe deposit box. Make a list of the names of the companies and the policy numbers and keep that in the box (in case a fire totally destroyed your home), but keep the actual policies at home.

6

Home, Sweet Home

Everyone may not "need" a sailboat, video recorder, sports car or other things that seem desirable to some—but everyone must have a place to live. There are expenditures relating to a physical place to reside which must be part of every budget. The amount spent on housing, furnishings, and maintenance says something about what we think is important, but everyone must make some outlay for housing.

As a member of the clergy, you may think you do not have a choice about whether to buy or rent a house. It may be that you have a house provided as part of your compensation, and you just take what is there. But as more church members become aware of the cost of housing, there are more options open to ministers than ever before. The two broad ways of dealing with clergy housing are either to provide a house the church owns as part of the salary or to give a housing allowance which the minister may use to rent or buy as he or she sees fit. We will first deal with the provided parsonage or manse.

There are many churches which own houses they bought years ago for very low prices compared to today's market, and they would have a hard time justifying giving up such houses to pay a housing allowance large enough to finance the same-size house today. In addition, some churches are located in areas where it would be difficult for ministers to arrange a quick resale of a house when they moved. Home ownership in that situation would be better for the church than for the pastor. However, there are still ways the church in those situations can help its minister enjoy the use of housing to achieve tax benefits and equity buildup, just as laymen do.

One of the best arrangements is one that several Lutheran

churches are using. The pastor lives in a church-owned house, but each year the church sets aside a percentage based on the pastor's salary (usually 1 percent to 3 percent) as an "equity allowance." It is the pastor's to take from church to church until he or she either goes to a church without a parsonage or retires. In either case, such ministers acquire some money for a down payment on a house of their own, even though they have lived in church-owned houses for years.

Another idea is to rent the church-owned house and turn over the rent to the pastor as a housing allowance to be used to rent a larger, smaller, or more suitable house, or buy one of his or her own.

There are a number of churches today which own houses (but would be glad not to) and would like to help the pastor get into a house of his own. These churches may sell the church-owned house to the pastor, taking a no-interest second note on the difference between what their affordable house allowance will finance and the new (usually higher) value of the house. The pastor makes little or no down payment. The second mortgage is paid when the pastor moves and/or sells the house (proceeds are then used to help the next minister get started in a house), or each year a part of the second mortgage is considered paid as part of his or her salary.

If a housing allowance is provided and there is no previously owned house in the current picture, the consideration will be whether to rent or buy a place to live. One argument for buying (that really has more to do with investments than housing) is that homes continually seem to be going up in value—and you had better buy now or you may not be able to later. Also, if you buy now, you will be increasing your actual equity, as inflation takes the value of the house higher than the price you paid for it. Those are good arguments, valid for many people but not for everyone. We will look at the situation as objectively as we can.

One consideration is where you are. What is the present market for houses, and what will it be in the future? Another consideration is the goals and achievements you have put on your lifeline. While you have to live somewhere, there are times when you may need to move on short notice, a freedom which home ownership may not provide. In that situation, if you live in an area where houses are slow to sell and you own a home, you will either have to move and leave an unsold house in another city or take a loss in order to get rid of it quickly. If people want to buy your house in a time when mortgage money is not easily available, they might not be able to qualify for a loan—and the only way you could sell would be to finance the note yourself. While this has some attractive qualities, it can still be a headache, especially if the buyers default and leave you with a house in a run-down condition. You are still stuck with making payments to a bank and repairing the house.

As you can see there are reasons not to buy a home just as valid as the ones for buying are. Look at your lifeline as it reflects your goals and values and predict whether or not you plan to be where you are for a long time. If you at least plan to stay put, and if business people in your area feel that there will be an influx of people looking for homes in the future or an increase in area population, buying will probably be a safe bet. If you are presently in a stable or declining area, buying may not be what is best for your plan, and renting may be a good alternative until you find the place where you want to live. Of course, if you plan to live in the area a long time, you may decide to buy anyway, just for the sake of being in a place you can do with as you please.

As will be mentioned in the chapter on credit, many lending agencies use a rule of thumb which says a reasonable amount to spend for purchasing a home is 28 percent of gross income. You still have to add utilities, repairs, and maintenance to that figure. If you cannot afford that much in your budget right now, buying is out for you, anyway, unless you consider some other alternatives. There are many older homes that can be bought at a deflated "as is" price and refurbished. They look bad to start with, but with a little work you can fix them up, sell them for a higher price, and then move up to a better house. You could do this if you have a little money right now, but you could also continue forever. I once knew a man who was very well off financially, but who did this even with very expensive houses.

Whether you buy or rent and whether you move from one house to another should be part of your planning, not just something that happens. Some friends of ours with two children had talked about how crowded their house was and how *"someday"* they planned to move to a larger one, probably in a few years. One day, however, they got to thinking that their children were already old enough to be leaving within just ten years, leaving the husband and wife alone in a big house. If they are going to move to a larger house for the comfort of the family, they must do it as soon as possible, or they might as well not do it at all. If they move, it may mean giving up something else right now, so the question has to be answered by looking at their lifeline plan and ranking priorities. Does the comfort of the family balance the sacrifice of what they would have to give up to buy a larger house now?

There are many things to consider in buying a house, especially if you use it as an investment or a tax shelter, and there are many books on just those subjects. I will not try to cover everything about the ins and outs of buying and owning, but merely point out that the decision must be a reflection of your life plans and not just something that happens spontaneously.

7

The Family Car

The need for transportation is an unavoidable fact of life. If you have an automobile which is used full- or part-time for church business, it is a lesser problem, because depreciation and other expenses on a business vehicle are tax deductible. But on the personal car that is used almost entirely for family purposes, the business calculations do not apply. It is the family car that will be considered here.

Just as in everything else, you can spend a little or a lot on family transportation, and the amount spent will reflect not only how much you can afford, but what you are saying about your values and goals. For good basic transportation, *Consumer Reports* recommends that you buy a car and drive it 100,000 miles and/or for ten years. (Most family cars average about 10,000 miles per year.) This makes the cost per mile about as low as possible, and gives you the most transportation for the money. If you start with a used car that is already two or three years old, this makes the cost per mile even less. If you also have a business automobile, you can do what many people do, drive it for two or three years until you have gotten the best tax advantage from it and then use it as your family car. The really good thing about this arrangement is that you will know exactly what shape your family car is in when you start using it that way.

One of the objections given for keeping a car for a long time is the increasing cost of repairs. However, when you figure the total cost of owning an automobile, it is almost always cheaper to keep an older car and repair it than to buy a new one. If owning a new car or a special kind of car (such as a van, pickup, four-wheel-drive vehicle) is part of your life goals, then admit it—but do not rationalize your buying a new car (and diverting money which could go for other things) as an economy measure, because it is not.

For example, insurance costs more on a newer car than an older one. And payments on a new car ultimately cost more than even high repair costs, unless you have let your older car go totally to pot before fixing what is wrong with it. Here's an example: The question is whether to buy a new car which sells for $6,000 and trade in your old car (worth $1,500), or keep the old car another three years and really fix it up. What are the arguments you might use to justify buying a new car? Better gas mileage? Cost of repairing the older car? You need a bigger car for your large family? Your values rank camping as a high priority, and you want a van to make camping easier and more comfortable? Maybe you just have the new-car bug?

If you have a car that is already paid for, the only costs that are now factors are repairs and maintenance and the extra cost of gasoline for a low-mileage car compared with a higher-mileage one. Even new cars have some repairs and maintenance, so we are really talking about the difference between those costs for an older car and a new one.

Let us assume the older car is in good shape in the body (not rusted, and so on). If you trade it in on the $6,000 car and get $1,500 on the trade-in, you will be left with $4,500 to finance. If the finance company or bank charges you 12 percent interest for three years, the monthly payments will be $150. For the sake of illustration, we will ignore all other costs except repairs and gasoline.

If you project the repairs on the old car as a constant (averaged for a year) of one-half the payments on the new car, repairs would be $75 per month or $900 for the year—as opposed to $1,800 in payments for the new car (assuming it needs no repairs, although that may not be the case). To break even, you would have to get a new car which would save you $900 in gasoline costs. The figures on the next page (Table 2) show gasoline costs for various mileage averages. If you assume that your car is used exactly 10,000 miles per year and gets the worst mileage on the chart (10 miles per gallon), you would have to buy a car which got even better mileage than the chart shows in order to save $900 on gasoline at two dollars a gallon.

There are other factors to be considered. On the positive side for buying a new car is the higher value it has over the older one, the bother of having to take the older one in for regular repairs, and the possible need for a bigger (or at least different) car for such good

Table 2

Gas Mileage/Gallons/Cost

This table is based on driving 10,000 miles. If you drive more or less than that per year, find the figures for your car for 10,000 miles and add or subtract the appropriate percentage. (For example: 12,000 miles per year would mean that you would add 20 percent to the 10,000-mile figure for your mileage/gallons/cost.)

Miles per Gallon	Gallons per 10,000 Miles	Costs for Varying Price per Gallon							
		$1.25	$1.50	$1.75	$2.00	$2.25	$2.50	$2.75	$3.00*
10.0	1,000	1,250	1,500	1,750	2,000	2,250	2,500	2,750	3,000
12.5	800	1,000	1,200	1,400	1,600	1,800	2,000	2,200	2,400
15.0	667	833	1,000	1,166	1,334	1,500	1,666	1,833	2,001
17.5	588	735	882	1,029	1,176	1,323	1,470	1,617	1,764
20.0	500	625	750	875	1,000	1,125	1,250	1,375	1,500
22.5	444	555	666	777	888	999	1,110	1,221	1,332
25.0	400	500	600	700	800	900	1,000	1,100	1,200
27.5	364	455	546	637	728	819	910	1,001	1,100
30.0	333	416	499	582	666	749	832	915	999
32.5	307	384	461	538	614	691	768	845	921
35.0	286	357	429	500	572	643	715	786	858
37.5	267	334	401	468	534	601	668	734	801
40.0	250	312	375	437	500	562	625	697	750

*If gasoline is higher than $3.00 per gallon, add the columns that equal the higher price. (Example: For $3.50 per gallon, add columns for $2.00 and $1.50.)

reasons as a growing family. Just the idea of "newness" is not a good reason to buy one. Look at your goals in life, the objectives you wish to achieve, and see how you can put as much money as possible toward those goals and as little as necessary into the family car, yet still have a dependable means of transportation.

8

Saving and Investing
for the Future

The purpose of insurance is to cover an unpredictable and devastating financial blow inflicted by some catastrophe that may occur in the future. Most persons, by purchasing insurance, are somewhat prepared for unknown disasters. But how do you handle major expenditures such as a house, a car, or a television set? Such purchases should also be planned. Perhaps you will have to anticipate borrowing money—almost always necessary when buying a house. But down payments on a house or car can be accumulated considerably in advance of the actual purchase. Provision can even be made for minor emergencies not covered by insurance or for the deductible amount on your insurance policies. The key to meeting such needs is a planned savings program. Savings, too, can be budgeted for certain foreseen expenses.

Even before all other obligations are met, there should be some money put aside for savings and investments for your future needs. You may have a budgeting problem which will first require getting some priority items paid before putting much into this area, but savings should be the number-two item in the budget after your tithe to the church. There is a classic book on this subject which was written as if an archaeologist had dug up writings from ancient Babylon. That book, by George S. Clason, is entitled *The Richest Man in Babylon.* Do not be put off by the title. It is a book filled with wisdom in the area of savings. The author suggests that we give a 10 percent tithe to ourselves *before* paying debts and even buying groceries. Clergy who stress a tithe to the church should understand this principle, but many people who give a tithe to God and a quarter of their earnings for income taxes do not do a good job of contributing to their own and their family's future through systematic savings.

Of course, you may protest that there is nothing left over for savings and investments after all the bills are paid. Many years ago, C. Northcote Parkinson became famous for Parkinson's Law, which dealt with such things as efficiency in government and bureaucracy in general. A few years later, he applied his findings to the household budget with what he called Mrs. Parkinson's Law. The principle here is that no matter how much money you make, expenses rise to meet income to the point where you always need just a hundred dollars more a month to get by comfortably. That is the point of assigning one-tenth to your savings-and-investment plan *before* you pay your VISA bill or buy clothing or food. Since we tend to spend to the limit of our resources, if we start out with 10 percent less, we will spend 10 percent less (again, assuming that we have first given 10 percent to God, so "our" 10 percent is really second).

Accessible Savings

The first place to put money for savings is in such readily accessible places as a passbook savings account in a bank, savings and loan association, or credit union. Another good depository is a NOW account, an arrangement whereby you have free checking and other bank services if you maintain a certain minimum balance, as well as receiving interest on your money. There are sources of higher interest, such as money-market funds, which will be discussed later.

A rule of thumb which many investment people recommend is that the ideal savings account would equal three months' salary. If you have adequate disability insurance, you could arrange to have disability insurance payments start three months *after* you are disabled. Premiums are cheaper on such a plan than on one that starts paying sooner. If you have three months' wages in savings that can be withdrawn in a hurry, you will be able to survive until the disability payments start coming. Besides the three months' wages, you could keep in savings an amount equal to the deductibles on your auto, home, medical, and/or health insurance.

Investment Philosophy

After you have accumulated three months' wages in a savings account of some kind (or sooner if you do not wish to wait that long), start putting money in investments, a way to make more money with the money put into them. If you like to fish and you buy a new fishing boat, you list that under the hobby part of your budget. Unless you are really willing to sell it on a moment's notice when there is a chance to make some money, you cannot label the purchase an investment.

Investments can be either fairly secure with almost no possibility of loss (such as United States Savings Bonds) or highly risky (such as speculative land purchases or trading commodities). The type of investments you choose should reflect your unique values and goals as you worked them out in chapter 3. Usually, the higher the risk, the higher the possibility of either high return or loss. With a low risk, the return is usually low as well. If you have enough extra money, you may want to put some of it in really secure investments and some in more risky ones in hopes of getting a higher return. But I would advise against putting any money into high-risk ventures if you cannot afford to lose it. That way, if all you do is break even or lose, you will only be disappointed, not badly hurt. There is nothing that is totally safe and without some risk, but you can find investments that are relatively secure, if that is what you want.

In what should you invest? Consider your goals and values. You may want to invest in things that reflect your values (if you are committed to something like physical fitness, you might want to invest in companies on the stock market that provide fitness equipment). If you do not want to make a statement of values in the area of investments, but just want to make money, there are other considerations.

You are probably familiar with the name Dow from the Dow-Jones stock averages. Many years ago, Charles Dow advanced a theory which described the stock market, but which also covered many other kinds of investments. Since he dealt with stocks, we will use that illustration. In theory, if a company had $100,000,000 in assets and had 10,000,000 shares of stock in the hands of stockholders, the real value of the stock (not counting such things as goodwill and other intangibles) would be $10 per share. But, in reality, the reputation of the company and other factors *do* come into play on the stock market. People's feelings about the company's products, the way it pays dividends, and so on, affect what people are willing to pay for the stock, regardless of its "real" value. Dow believed that for every stock (and I feel for any other investment) there is a real value and another value which people are willing to pay, sometimes higher than the real value, sometimes lower. Dow's theory of investment recommended studying the area in which you are considering investing until you think you know the real value of items in that area (in his case, stocks). If you do not have the time and/or the expertise to do that, find a reliable investment counselor knowledgeable in that area. Someone who is doing well in that investment field might recommend an advisor you can trust. Once you feel good about your knowledge or your advice, purchase those investments which seem to be selling at less than their real value. Then watch the market indications for those investments and sell when the price goes higher than the real value. When you have sold one investment and there are no investments at the moment which look underpriced, put the proceeds from the sale into fixed-interest investments—such as certificates of deposit or tax-free bonds—until something you might like to buy goes below its real value. That is basically the Dow theory, and I think it is a good one to use as a beginning philosophy with which to work.

There is a twofold problem with any investment (unless you just put your money in and forget it until you are ready to retire). The first is that people get greedy. Although the stock or other investment they bought below real value rises above its real value, they keep waiting until it "goes just a little bit higher." There is always a point at which the public loses interest in a stock or other investment, and the price goes down. Sometimes it goes down very rapidly! If you have been greedy and have been waiting for it to go just a little bit higher, you might wake up one morning and find your investment has fallen to below its real value, and maybe even below your purchase price. According to Dow's theory, if you hang on to it, it may eventually go back up, but you will have still lost time and other investment opportunities. Time is money! So do not be greedy. With any investment, pick a sell price in advance, so you will not be tempted to hang on just a little longer in the heat of a rising market.

The other problem area for the investor is to fall in love with an investment. This is similar to investment greed, but instead of hanging on to the investment and waiting for the price to go higher, the lover hangs on forever. An example is an investor who buys gold and is obsessed with the very idea of owning gold, rather than in its investment potential. There might be a right time to buy gold (or make any other investment), but there is also a time to sell, and the lover may be in even worse shape than the greedy investor. Remember, investments are really long-term savings which are just one part of the budget you are using to reflect your goals and values in life. In looking at your answer in chapter 3 about what you would like to have achieved in your life time, how will your use of investments reflect those goals?

Acquiring Investment Know-How

Many ministers do not have the time to deal on a daily, weekly, or even a monthly basis with rising and falling investment markets, nor do they have time to study enough to become investment experts. It is not necessary to be an expert; just get a basic knowledge of investments (which does take a little time) and then find a good financial advisor. The best single book I have found on investing in the stock market is *Dun and Bradstreet's Guide to Your Investments,* by C. Colburn Hardy. There are many other good books, but if you have time to read only one, that should be it.

Most good libraries have sections on investments and finances, with books on everything from real estate to diamonds. There are many books in the popular press that cover how to invest in crisis times and how to make money with inflation-proof investments. I have read a great number of these books, and my one-word summary of what I think the heart of what I have learned is: Diversify. "Don't put all your eggs in one basket," my father used to say. No single investment, from stocks to gold or real estate to oil wells, is so free of risk that you ought to put *all* your investment capital there.

How do you achieve diversification, with a good balance between a fairly secure return on your money and yet a reasonable high performance of your total investment package or portfolio? The first question you have to answer is how much time, energy, effort, and worry you are going to expend on the investment process. If your essential calling is to be a pastor, and you have almost no time to spend in supervising your investments; you either need to entrust your money to a sound financial manager and be happy with whatever he or she does for you—or invest in the lowest risk/lowest management investments, so that all you have to do is send money once a month. A good money-market fund, growth mutual fund, and/or cash value life insurance may be your best investment choices.

With little time to spend on investments, your foundation might be a program built on cash-value life insurance (the reason to be discussed later). If you already have such a base, but still do not want to have to worry about your investment package, pick a good mutual fund. There are many places to look for advice on which funds to buy. Again, try your local library. Magazines such as *Money* and *Changing Times* print periodic articles on good mutual funds. Check to see what Hardy says about mutual funds in *Dun and Bradstreet's Guide to Your Investments*.

Mutual Funds

A little information about mutual funds might be helpful for those who do not know much about them. A mutual fund takes small amounts of money from investors and uses this large pool to purchase stocks, bonds, government securities and notes (money markets), and so on. The management company which looks after the fund gets a small percentage of the assets each year (something like one-half of one percent, which makes them desire the fund's growth as much as you do. There are two types of mutual funds, relating to how the investment is purchased—load and no-load. In a no-load fund there may be a small fee to cover paperwork, but since there are no commissions paid to a stockbroker, these funds are usually not sold by brokers. A load fund has a commission deducted from each investment amount to pay the broker. Some people have the mistaken idea that it is always better to use a fund with no commissions to be paid so all the money would go into the investment. Whether it is a load or no-load fund has little to do with the success of the fund, as both types can be successful and both types can fail to grow. A load fund that grew would have been a better investment than a no-load that did not.

Most mutual funds have a specific purpose that guides their investment philosophy and purchases. They may specialize in growth stocks (which pay little dividends but increase in value) or income stocks (which may not rise but generally pay high dividends) or money markets (high-interest government and commercial paper, bonds, notes). A balanced fund would have both stocks and bonds. Some funds invest in only one area of the economy (for instance, food stores, utilities, and so on).

If you choose a mutual fund for your investment, many firms will let you invest a regular monthly amount in the fund, such as fifty dollars. The value of the fund will rise and fall during each month, but if you invest the money at the same time each month, you will have an average (called dollar-cost averaging) between the highs and lows. This method is supposed to be better than trying to buy the same number of individual stocks each month, regardless of cost.

Mutual funds can also be used as tax shelters. All mutual fund companies are not set up to handle tax shelters, so their funds would be called nonqualified. If yours can handle one, you have to qualify for either a Keogh (HR-10) or a 403(b) and/or an Individual Retirement Account (I.R.A.). For more information on tax shelters, see chapters 10 and 11.

Diversify Your Investments

If you have only a little to spend for investing, you will probably want to start with relatively low-risk ventures, later moving on to the more risky ones where the possibility of return is greater—but only if you can stand the loss, the chances for which are also greater. You might wish to combine an aptitude or interest with your investing. For example, if you like to tinker and repair things, a rental property might be an ideal investment, because you could save on repair expenses by doing them yourself. You might also fit a hobby like coin or stamp collecting into your investment portfolio. Diversity is still the main idea, however.

How diverse should your investments be? It depends on how much you intend to put to work for you. If you are just getting started, one dollar a month put into twenty-five investments is just not as practical as putting $25 per month into one, or perhaps $12.50 per month into two. Many investment vehicles such as mutual funds have minimum investment amounts, perhaps $50 per month. Start with one or two of the less risky investments that fit your goals and budget. Then, as you pay off prior debt, you can consider your overall plan and either put more into fairly secure investments because of your time limitation or your goal orientation—or more into the more risky areas.

If your investment offers a way to save on taxes, that is a bonus. Also, if some of your investments are aimed at retirement, those can be put into tax-sheltered plans (and should probably be the part of your portfolio with the least risk). Retirement planning is dealt with in another chapter, so we will not go further into that here.

For an example of an almost risk-free basic investment, consider a cash-value life insurance policy on which the dividends are used to purchase paid-up additions. (The only possible risks are the remote chance that the company might go out of business and that the economy would become so poor that the company would not be able to pay dividends.) Appendix F-1 to F-5 (already discussed in chapter 5) compares cash-value life insurance where dividends are used to purchase paid-up additions with the concept of buying term insurance and investing the cost differential. Although the charts are only for ages twenty-five, thirty, thirty-five, forty, and forty-five, they will give you the idea, whatever your age. The difference-invested method assumes a return and a tax payment according to a specific bracket. The value of the investments is net (all fees and commissions are paid), and losses are offset by enough gains to give an 8 percent return with a 25 percent tax bracket, a 10 percent return with a 40 percent tax bracket, or a 12 percent return with a 50 percent tax bracket. In every case, the cash value of the permanent life insurance exceeds the cash value of the investments and also provides increasing insurance protection and no investment-management problems. You merely send a premium check when due. This could be a good foundation for an investment plan on which to build and diversify. To reiterate, however, it has to be *your* plan, to fit your goals and dreams.

9

Using Credit Wisely

In the 1950s, Tennessee Ernie Ford had a hit song titled "Sixteen Tons." In it, there was a line which describes many people who use credit unwisely: "I owe my soul to the company store." In this day of plastic money, there is the constant temptation to buy now and pay later. When used with care, charge cards and other credit arrangements are very useful and can help in achieving long-term goals. But if you let the charging get out of hand, you will be surrendering control of your life and destiny to the credit-card company. You will literally owe your soul to someone other than God and yourself.

In planning a budget where use of money will demonstrate your goals and values, you must take into account your present debt(s). House payments were previously discussed, so we will not deal with them here. Instead, we will look at loans for cars and other major purchases—and the ever-present credit cards. When you plan your budget, earmark for the future some items you may want or even need. If you already owe for anything other than house, furniture, or car, enter that under Prior Debt Retirement. Even if you owe on five different accounts, lump them all together as of the date you intend to start a budget plan which will truly reflect your lifestyle. If you must charge on one of the accounts after that date, enter the amount in the pertinent category on the budget sheet. If you cannot afford to pay both the minimum payment for prior expenses plus the new charges, at least pay for the new items and the interest for that month. Although this will retain the prior debt, you will begin living according to your plan.

How much debt can you carry? Different experts give different advice. I have heard some bankers suggest that the annual house debt be no more than 28 percent of gross income (before taxes and other deductions are made from your paycheck). But they also say that an auto loan should probably be no more than 20 percent of *take home pay*. Assuming that you are buying a house and a car and stay within those percentages, many smart people say that all other debts should total no more than 25 percent of your income. That does not mean just charge cards! Those are good figures for bankers, but they may not be for you. Starting with those as maximum-debt allowables, you should look at your lifeline to decide if you might wish to set much lower maximums for yourself in some areas of debt, in order to accomplish the other things you wish to achieve.

If part of your investment strategy is to buy an income-producer such as rental property, the debt on that property is in a different category. Although it will produce income which must be accounted for, it should stand on its own as much as possible—any extra amount to be added by you as part of your regular monthly savings and investments. We are concerned here with your household debt. Business and investment debts have to be figured differently and will not be discussed in this chapter.

Once you have decided where you are going with your life and want to plan your management of money to reflect that, there may seem to be problems with prior debt. If you have already gotten into the position where previous expenses prevent new spending in an important area, just take that into account in your planning and live with it. If your budget is so tight that it is causing family arguments—because there is more month left over at the end of the paycheck than vice versa—you might consider either a consolidation loan, or going to your creditors and saying, "Look, we are in a bind, but I plan to pay you X amount of money a month until I owe you nothing." The creditors may complain and even threaten, but unless the debt is on something they can repossess, they will probably go along with you if you have a definite repayment plan and stick to it. Beware of consolidating present debt and then increasing that with more charges.

One question about debt is whether to use savings to pay off those bills. That can be answered only by considering your lifeline planning, how you feel about debt in general, and how much security you need in savings. Businesses have no problems justifying debt for capital expenditures with which they can increase income. Similarly, if you have a chance to go to school or do something else that will move you further along on your long-term plan, such spending might be easily justified as something for which it is worth going into debt. Replacement of major household items such as a refrigerator may be so large an expense that using credit may be the only way to do it without totally depleting savings. However, if your style of life and your negative attitude toward debt make you feel secure only when totally out of debt, using savings to pay off an obligation might be more consistent with your values—even if you must temporarily exhaust your reserves.

If you can live without getting ulcers while carrying some reasonable debt, plan your budget so that you can whittle away at the present debt while retaining adequate savings for emergency needs (see chapter 8 on savings and investments). In that way, you will not be caught with a need for cash when you have none available. Even so, look for ways to cut down on the interest and service charges you must pay for whatever debt you have outstanding. You might borrow money from a credit union or bank to pay off debts to department stores and other charge-card institutions which charge higher interest fees. The total amount of debt will not rise, but the amount of interest paid will be less, thus allowing you to spend more money in areas where your goals and values lie. A reminder: do not consolidate debt and then go out and charge more things on your credit cards without paying the total bill each month.

Future debt is something which can be of great benefit, if handled with care. From this point on, the way you handle both prior and future debt should reflect your goals, priorities, and values. If you have made a decision to move immediately in certain directions with your life, but cannot because of prior debt commitments (and consolidation is not wise for you because you might be tempted to charge again), there is another option. Decide to assign the money presently involved in debt retirement into your goal areas, just as soon as you pay off some creditor. For example, suppose you now owe Sears $25 per month, VISA $36 per month, Master Card $46 per month, and some other loan agency $60 per month for a refrigerator. With many credit card companies, as your overall balance goes down, so does your minimum monthly payment. There are two ways to accomplish paying off your old debt and converting those dollars to directions that reflect your chosen lifestyle. One would be to budget the total amount now owed (in the example,

$167 per month), and as the balances and minimum payments of the accounts go down, simply put the difference into your important areas. *So long as you do not charge more,* the monthly debt retirement would get smaller and the amount going into the new areas of budget would increase.

The second method of changing your pattern would be to budget so that you continue to pay Sears, VISA, and so on at the same rate you are now, even though their minimums would be going down. This would mean you would be paying them off faster. If you do this, the various creditors will probably be paid off at different times. Assuming from our example that the lowest monthly payment meant the lowest total debt, as time passed you could pay off Sears and next month immediately put $25 into new areas which reflect your life plan. Next, VISA would be paid off, and you could add $36 per month to a priority category, and so on. What matters most is not which method you use, but that you deal with your present debt in a constructive way which begins to let your budget bring you closer to your dreams and aspirations.

10

Social Security and Other Tax Considerations

For social security purposes only, clergy are considered self-employed persons. Unless you opted out of the system during the first two years after you were ordained, commissioned, or licensed, you must pay social security contributions on income earned as a minister (IRS Publication 517). If, however, you are within the first two years of ordination, you have the option to request exemption on income earned as a minister. (You must still pay social security on other salaried income—as a teacher, for example—that is not directly related to your ordination and services as a minister.) You must apply for such an exemption on IRS Form 4361, and you must be doing so for other than economic reasons (you can't just not want to spend the money). What you must sign on the form is that you are conscientiously opposed to acceptance of the benefits of any public insurance *because of your religious principles.* If you sign such a document and are ever audited, you must satisfactorily convince the auditor that your religious principles are why you opted out of the program. Otherwise, the auditor can require that you enter the program and pay social security contributions and penalties for the previous three years.

Remember, this applies only to income earned as a minister. If you have worked before ordination, or have any other kind of employment after being ordained, you must still pay social security contributions on that income and can receive retirement and other benefits based on what you have contributed, once minimums have been reached. If you are past two years of ordination, you have no choice anyway; you must pay the contributions.

If you have elected to opt out of the system, how do you prove that you did so on religious grounds? Besides having a good theological argument, it helps to have set up your own insurance and retirement plan that will duplicate the benefits which social security would have provided. A good insurance agent can calculate what you would lose in social security benefits and what kind of private insurance program would replace the death, disability, and retirement features lost when you opted out. Since the benefits change almost yearly, I will not try to go into detail here. If you wish to have more specific information, you may call or write your nearest IRS office and ask for Publication 517 and Form 4361.

When calculating social security payments, there are varying opinions about whether to include the value of housing (either a parsonage or an allowance). An interpretation of IRS Codes, backed by an opinion of the Supreme Court, is that housing provided for an employee for the benefit of the employer is not reportable as income for social security purposes. At the time of this writing, there have been no court cases to test the subtle interpretations of this rule, but it is my opinion that if a housing allowance is for a minister's benefit (that he or she wants to own a house is the primary reason a housing allowance is given), housing must then be included for social security purposes. If the parsonage or housing allowance is given because that is what the church/employer wishes, it is my opinion that the housing value or allowance not be included in social security calculations. Since this is only my opinion, you should check with your tax advisor for clarification.

Income tax calculations are another matter. For income tax, ministers are *not* considered self-employed, therefore cannot have the tax shelters available to self-employed persons under the HR-10 or Keogh plans (see IRS Publication 560). The unique aspect of income tax for ministers is that a part of housing allowances can probably be tax-sheltered. A minister may not deduct from taxable income the portion of real estate taxes and other housing costs that is proportionally the same as his or her housing allowance is to entire salary, but he or she may exclude reporting the housing allowance itself. See Appendix H for sample calculations of this point.

While ministers are not eligible for Keogh plans, they may take advantage of a tax shelter that is available to all employees of schools, churches, and nonprofit organizations. If you do not have a pension plan with your denomination, you may start your own plan, called a 403(b) plan, and contribute up to 16.67 percent of your salary to this pension. See IRS Publication 571 for detailed discussion of 403(b). If you do have a denominational plan, you may also have a 403(b) plan for yourself, but the contributions to both the denominational plan and your own may not total more than 25 percent. For example, if your denominational plan took 15 percent of your salary, the 403(b) contribution could be only 10 percent. However, if the denominational contribution was only 5 percent, you still could not put more than 16.67 percent into the 403(b), even though the total is less than 25 percent. Since 1982, everyone may also have an Individual Retirement Account (I.R.A.) and contribute up to $2,000 per working adult in the family (or up to total income if it was less than $2,000 per year). If you can afford only one plan, however, choose the 403(b), because there is no penalty for early withdrawal of funds as there is with the I.R.A. (you must pay taxes due on withdrawal for both, but with an I.R.A. there is also a 10 percent early withdrawal penalty).

Tax-sheltering is provided by both an I.R.A. and a 403(b), which is called that for the pertinent paragraph number is the IRS Code (the IRS uses paragraph numbers as we in the church use chapter and verse for Bible references). This means that part of your income is sheltered or exempt from taxes for the present. Taxes are not paid until later in life, usually after retirement, when you will probably be in a lower tax bracket. The way a tax shelter works is easy to understand. Looking at the chart below, you can see that as income rises there is a point at which taxes must be paid. So long as you do not make enough to cross the tax line, you pay no income tax. When your income crosses the line, taxes are due on a graduated scale. The more income reported, the greater the percentage going to income tax. The concept of a tax shelter is that you find ways the IRS sanctions which allow you not to report part of your income, thus reducing or eliminating income taxes because your income level is lower with reference to the tax line. Another type of tax shelter gives tax credits, which means that even if your income crosses the line, after you figure the amount of your tax, you can subtract credits directly from the tax that would otherwise be due. Examples of each type shelter are (1) money put into a retirement plan such as a 403(b) for keeping the taxable income down, and (2) the investment tax credit you get when you itemize deductions and purchase a new car to be used for work.

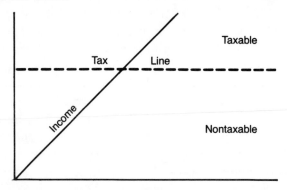

How do you make the most of clergy tax advantages? First, have all reasonable items designated as allowances which are not reportable (such as a housing allowance). Next, put as much as you can afford into a 403(b) up to the maximum allowable and also into an I.R.A. If you still show enough taxable income to owe a tax, ask investment advice from a broker or financial advisor. You may learn how to purchase tax shelters that will exactly offset the tax amount (such as oil-exploration ventures, cable TV expansion, equipment rental partnerships, and so on). If the money would otherwise be spent on taxes, you have no reason not to use that money for investments in ways that the I.R.S. says are allowable.

An elder in a church where I was once pastor thought that doing anything to avoid taxes was immoral. It most certainly is not! The government allows tax shelters for a reason, and so long as you obey the law and invest accordingly, there is nothing immoral about it. Tax shelters such as mentioned are designed to give the economy a boost by putting money to work where it will eventually generate even more taxes. When you invest in a 403(b) or an I.R.A., you are putting money into the hands of insurance companies, banks, stock companies, and so on. They use that money to build factories, office buildings, and more, thus helping the general economy and generating more taxes for the government to collect later. It is still true that the only things that are certain are death and taxes. If you avoid some taxes through legal means, there are usually more taxes to be collected somewhere else because of it.

11

Planning for Retirement

The younger you are, the less you usually think you need to be concerned about retirement. You live today without being anxious about tomorrow. While you should not worry too much about age sixty-five when you are only twenty-five, even fifty, you should plan well for the future to see that everything on your lifeline can be carried out, including retirement. The younger you start on retirement investments, the better and more comfortably you will live in retirement. Of course, that has to be balanced against today's needs, but retirement planning should not be entirely ignored just because of current necessities.

Most major denominations in the United States have pension plans for their clergy. These are almost always tax-sheltered plans, which means that your contributions are deducted from taxable income today, although you will pay taxes on the money received during retirement. As mentioned in the previous chapter, you can supplement your retirement with a personal plan, 403(b), and also an I.R.A. If you are contributing to social security, you can hope to receive benefits from that or from a similar program when you retire. But will all these be enough?

That is a question that can be personalized by looking at the lifeline plan you made earlier. If you wish to make an annual trip to the Holy Land after retirement, you will need more money than if you plan to sit by a stream, fishing the rest of your life away.

One major need in retirement is a place to live. If you are in a denomination where almost all the churches own the houses in which their ministers live, you will need to begin saving and investing now in such ways that will allow you to buy a house when

73

you retire or else realize enough from your retirement income to make rent payments. For many years, some ministers have used cash-value life insurance as a way to take care of future housing, acquiring enough insurance to allow their families to have a paid-for home in the event of their own early death. If they survive until retirement age, the cash value may be used to purchase a home or make a healthy down payment. For those fortunate enough to be pastoring in churches which allow them to be buying a home now, that area is already cared for.

Another concern for the future is outliving your retirement income. If you have invested in securities, real estate, and so on, and start cashing in these assets and living off the proceeds when you retire, the money may eventually run out, especially if your expenses are increased by costly medical bills. There are several ways to handle this problem. One is to invest in an annuity, which is handled by an insurance company and guarantees a certain income for your life, or for your life and that of your spouse, or for a fixed number of years such as ten or twenty. In the latter case, if you and your spouse both die, another beneficiary gets the money for the prescribed number of years. Annuities can be tax-sheltered (called qualified plans) and contributed to through the years as part of your retirement program, so that at age sixty-five you simply choose which way you wish to receive your payments. You could take them in a lump sum but that is not such a wise move for tax purposes. If you reach retirement age and have a large amount of cash from stocks or real estate or whatever, you can then purchase an annuity which will give you the same options—guaranteed income for life or a certain number of years.

You can take another look at the charts in Appendix G, to see how much capital you would need to provide specified incomes for varying numbers of years. These figures work whether you are looking at insurance need or retirement need. The most important chart for me is Figure G-2, which shows that you can protect against inflation by not spending the entire amount that you receive each year from investment. Instead, you reinvest some all the time. That will protect against inflation. What about deflation? While it is true that we have had more inflation than deflation through the years, a well-rounded financial plan would protect against both. That is why any retirement program ought to include some type of annuity with a guaranteed minimum. Most insurance companies provide guaranteed minimums, but they are currently paying much higher than the minimums and probably always will, unless the economy goes into a deflationary period. If you have chosen a sound company, its investments are such that they can always pay their minimums, even in the worst of times.

Choosing an insurance company from a stability-and-safety standpoint is fairly easy. There is an independent rating company called A. M. Best. Many good libraries will have their publications or can get them for you—or your insurance agent can tell how A. M. Best rates his or her company. The ratings are like school grades: $A+$ down to C. They are not a judgment of how worthy the company is or whether its products are expensive or inexpensive, but rather make a statement about the financial condition of the company, especially its ability to pay future claims. Since there are thousands of insurance companies in the United States, there is no reason not to deal with one of the several hundred that have an A. M. Best rating of A or $A+$. There are also other rating companies; just be sure that their top ratings are equal to A. M. Best's A or $A+$.

There are several reasons for having an annuity as an investment base when planning for retirement. One is that it is an investment that protects against both inflation and deflation, while many others do not. But even more important is that an annuity gives you a more or less definite rate of return for certain periods of time, so that you can predict what you will have at the end of your investing years. Suppose you can put $1,000 per year into an annuity currently paying 10 percent. Looking at Appendix I, you can find in the 10 percent column (opposite the number of years until you retire) the amount of money which will be there at retirement. Stocks, real estate, and most other investments do not yield this type of easily predicted totals, as they are subject to so many variables. The explanations in Appendix I also show how to figure the value of your annuity each time the company sends you a notice that they have changed their interest rate.

Appendix J gives some illustrations of what can be done with $1,200 per year. If all you want is an annuity, use Appendix I and multiply the figures by 1.2 to see how much $1,200 would provide by retirement. However, if you would like to add a little extra protection to the plan, use the suggestion given in Appendix J and put part of the money toward an insurance policy. The five illustrations use an annually renewable term policy (which provides

$100,000 as cheaply as possible at any age), then freezes the premiums after two years on the older persons' policies, or when the premiums reach $200 on the younger persons' policies—thus turning them into decreasing-term policies. When the annuity benefit nears $100,000, the policies are dropped entirely. This program should not be a replacement for an adequate insurance program as described in chapter 5, but should be seen as additional protection for your retirement plans.

More and more people reach retirement age with a large enough amount of money to require special estate planning. Whether you inherit money or just do well on investments in times of inflation, if you reach age sixty-five with a large estate, Appendix K may be of help to you, as it suggests a plan for estate distribution.

12

Questions and Answers and a Few Suggestions

Q: *How much time will it take each month to do the paperwork involved in the back of this book?*

A: Parkinson's Law suggests that people tend to fill whatever time is available to them. If you sit down with two hours to kill, you could easily use up the two hours. But if you are the type who can sit down and get right to business and get it over with, it should not take very long. Of course, at first, until you become familiar with the worksheets and what items go into which categories, it will take what seems like a long time. However, after you have kept the records for a while, and put items on the worksheets as you pay bills or on some regular schedule, it will not take much time compared with the benefits you will gain.

Q: *If I do all the things suggested in this workbook, how long will it take for the plan to really work in my financial life?*

A: That cannot be answered in a general way, because different people will be at different places as they read this book. Some may already have done financial and life planning without even being aware of it, so they might be able to start immediately using the worksheets to discover where they are right now. Others might be deeply in debt and have to wait as much as a year or more to pay off those debts before they can even begin to save or put money into their priority items. However, if they make the decision to start paying off those debts, the plan begins working immediately for them from the moment the plan is put into action. It may take a while to see results, but it will work for you, too.

Q: *If I were good at record keeping, I would probably have done most of this work already and would have a routine established. How much time do I have to spend doing this before it will work?*

A: As I have explained, the monthly time will vary, but the minimum length of time to make the plan work well is three years. That may sound like a long time, but it really is not. Once the plan is working, you really should keep at the routine all the rest of your life. If the plan seems to be working well, there may be a temptation to stop, especially if you just do not enjoy record keeping. However, if you are serious about being in control of your life, it will require at least a minimum amount of discipline. When you first start, it may seem as if a lot of hours are being spent on the process, but as you get used to doing it, you can adapt. Perhaps you might begin by working on the worksheet weekly and over time evolve a schedule which requires filling in the blanks only once a month or even once every two months. The main thing is to stick with it!

Q: *You include allowances in the budget. Is that just for the children?*

A: No matter how tight a budget is and how small the allowance has to be, all family members ought to have at least a little money they can spend any way they wish. It may be enough for only a soft drink or a magazine, but it is theirs alone. As the budget grows, allowances can also increase. Children's allowances can be a way to teach them to do what the adult members are doing with lifeline planning. Teach them to save a little from each allowance until they have enough to get something special and go on from there.

Q: *Is there any way to save money on what we have to buy?*

A: There are several ways—and many good books and articles have been written on that subject. Using coupons is one way to save, but finding and organizing them uses time, and sometimes a store brand is just as good and less expensive than using a cents-off coupon on a name brand. Do you have the time and are you saving enough to make using coupons worthwhile? If the answer is yes, then you ought to use them.

I usually go to the library and look at *Consumer Reports* magazine before I buy any major item. Often the most expensive model is not the best buy. The magazine also gives opinions based on testing they have done, and whether you agree or disagree, they usually tell what to look for when making major (and even minor) purchases.

Speaking of the library, if you are like most people, you get a lot of advertisements in the mail for book clubs. If you use the library instead, or at least go to used-book stores, you can read the most popular books at no charge or cheaper than the book clubs. Another opportunity for savings is on food and other items from the supermarket. If you know how much soap, toilet paper, detergents, for example, you use in a month or even a year, you can buy large quantities when those things are on sale. This will be cheaper than just picking up the items everytime you run out. The same is true for nonperishable food items. The Civil Defense Agency recommended several years ago that everyone ought to have a minimum of a two-week supply of food and water and other items for such emergencies as natural disasters in which supplies might be interrupted temporarily. When most people lived on farms, they stored enough food to last from one season to the same season next year, equivalent to a whole year's supply of food. Some people still advocate that policy (including the Mormon Church or the Church of Jesus Christ of Latter Day Saints). Canned goods and dried food can be stored in a cool place and used over a period of time. It makes good sense in a time of inflation, anyway, to buy all you can afford of commonly used items and use them six months later, when their price may be even higher. Most canned and dried foods need to be rotated, so don't put them in the closet and forget them. Those who really get serious about long-term storage even stockpile raw wheat and dehydrated foodstuffs such as campers carry into the backwoods. If you are interested in such storage, get a good book from your library on the subject or consult the Mormon Church. You can get lists of recommendations from the Civil Defense Agency or from books, but it is best to make your own list of goods that you usually eat. Buy them in large quantities when on sale and use them out of the closet when they are not. I believe money taken from savings to set up a food-storage plan is really just shifting the savings dollars from the bank to the pantry. We do it, and I highly recommend it.

Some people think they will save money by buying a food freezer. If you can get meat cheaply by buying a half or quarter section you may save money, but you have to figure in the cost of the freezer and electricity when considering how much you are really saving. For some people it works and for others it does not.

Q: *What about cable television? Does it save money on entertainment?*

A: People who like to go to the movies might find that cable television with Home Box Office, Showtime, or other movie channels might save them money, but only if they stay home to watch TV and quit going to the movie theater. The real question about cable television is not so much the money angle, but how sitting in front of the TV fits your lifestyle and life plan. If going to the theater is not just for the entertainment of watching a film, but is also a way to get out, see people, and interact with the audience, cable television would not supply that need, even though it might be saving you money.

A broader question is how watching television fits your family's life plan. Should you be developing relationships, going to school, working on a hobby, or doing things with your children instead of sitting in front of the TV? Television can be a great educational and entertainment tool if it is controlled by you and not the other way around. I once heard a man call in to a radio show to say that he was once addicted to TV, watching every waking moment he was not at work—until one day it dawned on him that the people he watched on TV were always doing more interesting and exciting things than sitting in front of a TV set. It does not have to be an either/or situation. Watch TV, including cable television, when you feel it is worthwhile, but choose other activities at other times. Cable television is just now coming of age, and there are more things available than just movies and sports. You may regard some service that is provided as something that fits your life plan (a computer hookup, medical and fire alerts, and special educational opportunities such as college courses on the local access channel). The question is still: Does the money spent on this service reflect how your family ought to be spending money in order to get where they are heading, do what they plan to accomplish, and be what they want to be?

Q: *Do we need to insure our children?*

A: For medical needs, definitely. Any life insurance should cover at least the cost of a funeral and perhaps such things as deductibles on medical insurance. I know of a family whose child died of leukemia. The medical insurance covered only 80 percent of the hospital and doctor bills, so they were grateful for the life insurance to help pay the difference. Life insurance is normally expected to replace the income that would be lost if one of the wage earners of the family were to die. Children are to be loved and appreciated but, realistically, they provide no income to the family. It is generally better to spend the money to insure the parents. If the children are still young and the mother does not work outside the home, it is important for her to have life insurance, so that child care could be covered in the event of her death. You should insure against not just lost income but also lost service to the family.

Some salesmen will try to get you to buy life insurance on your children by guaranteeing a low, low rate for a two-year-old that a twenty-one-year-old could not get. Or that you ought to purchase an insurance policy that will mature and provide money for college when they reach that age. The salesman is correct about the rates, but both parents ought to be fully insured before getting more than a minimum on the children. An excellent rider for children's insurance is an option to purchase more insurance in the future, regardless of health. If your budget will allow you to purchase for your children either a $10,000 policy with no riders, or a $5,000 policy with an option to purchase up to $100,000 in the future, take the latter.

Q: *Should both the husband and wife have wills?*

A: Definitely! Even though you are doing your lifeline planning as if you will live until at least eighty years of age, people of all ages are killed in accidents or die from sudden illness. Especially if there are minor children, the will should deal not only with money matters but also the guardianship of the children. It is advisable for both husband and wife to have wills. Do not keep them in your safe deposit box, as in many states access to a safe deposit box is restricted for some time after death. Keep a copy there, but also have a copy at home where everyone in the family knows where it is. While in most states a simple handwritten will is valid, it is worth the expense to have a lawyer draw one up for you.

Q: *If one of the adults in the family dies, how does that affect our life plan?*

A: First, in the case of death, use the checklist (Appendix L) to guide you when someone dies. Besides the immediate cares and concerns relating to the funeral, there are financial matters to resolve, especially after the loss of a spouse. Since life must eventually go on, at a time no more than a month or two after the funeral, it would be advisable to sit down and reevaluate your assets and liabilities. Then look at what is necessary to get on with living. Make no major decisions (such as selling the house) until the shock of the death has worn off, which may take only a few months or as much as a year. Do not make decisions alone. Talk with a lawyer, counselor, another minister, or someone else you can trust to listen and react to your ideas.

Q: *What if I have questions about social security benefits?*

A: Any question you have can be answered at the nearest social security office. Since benefits change almost annually, it would be a good plan to go down to an office at least every ten years and ask them what the current benefits are. It is also a good idea to verify every three years that you are receiving proper credit for the money you are paying into the system. A computer mistake or human error could accidentally credit one or more years of your payments to someone else's account, and the sooner that is caught the better. There is a postcard available at your local social security office that can be sent in for just that purpose.

Q: *I would like to do a lot of things, and our lifeline planning reflects that, but it turns out to be more than just a question of money—there is also the question of time. How do I manage my time as well as my money?*

A: If you are really interested in something, you tend to work it into your schedule, even if you have to drop something else. I once read that most people have time for only about five major commitment areas. Assuming that your job is one, a second is a minimum amount of time spent with your family (not just being in the house, but playing, talking, and sharing activities with your spouse and children). That leaves three major time-commitment slots for education, hobbies, PTA, scouting, fishing, building your mountain cabin retreat, and so on. Don't overcommit your time any more than you would overcommit your money. If you do not have immediate money to put into some area, budgeting time for it may be a way to demonstrate that commitment, even before you can invest your funds in it.

Q: *How do I handle unforeseen happenings, such as illness or inheriting money?*

A: You may face an unexpected major event at least once in your life, but the worst thing is that you might have to change your basic life plan. Having a plan helps you avoid spur-of-the-moment decisions made without really thinking things through. A friend may have a great business opportunity which he wishes to share with you. Your decision should be based on your total life plan rather than on just friendship. A real friend will not mind if you show him that the reason you cannot participate in this great deal with him is that it does not fit your long-term goals. If something upsets your plan, just sit down and go through the process again, making adjustments accordingly.

Q: *Should a wife work?*

A: Since most wives work, the question is whether wives should work *outside the home.* Look at your lifeline and your theology. What are the family goals? If you place a high value on family and children, perhaps it would be better for the wife to remain home than to be out earning money. The first five to six years are when children learn basic values. The time that a mother (and when possible, the father) spends with young children is worth more than money. Perhaps the wife could stay home until the children are in school and then go to work. For some people, this may not be an option. If bills have to be paid and one salary is not enough, the mother may have to work. But when there is a choice, it should not be based on emotion. One important consideration that may not be stated on the lifeline is that sometimes a wife has a career goal just as her husband does. Her needs must be met, and money is not really the entire question. Discuss with the whole family just what it would mean for Mother to have a job. Decide after examining the family's life plan.

Q: *I have some ideas for things that you have not mentioned and some questions you have not answered? What do I do?*

A: Write to me. I am always open to new ideas and will be glad to try to answer any question I can, or ask an expert so that we can both learn. My address is:

> David L. Northcutt
> 9902 Windriver
> Houston, TX 77070

Q: *What if I like this plan so well that I want to continue using the worksheets indefinitely. Where do I get more?*

A: If you have purchased this book for yourself, you may photo-copy the worksheets *for your own use.* Although copyright laws say you cannot copy someone else's material and sell it for profit, you may make copies for your personal use.

13

Putting It All Together

Now that you have gone this far, it is time to reflect on and organize the information into a workable system. If you wish to follow everything in this workbook, here is the order in which it ought to be done. (Put a check beside each step as you accomplish that item.)

_____ 1. Complete the "Where Are You Now?" chart (Appendix B).

_____ 2. Complete the "Where Are You Going?" lifeline (Appendix C). It might be helpful to read through the appropriate paragraphs of Sample Situations and Strategies (Appendix N). This section covers some illustrative planning for a single person, as well as for married couples of different ages. The material might spark your thinking or give you some fresh ideas.

_____ 3. Set up the monthly budget worksheets (Appendix D).

_____ 4. Begin a regular savings plan.

_____a. Put aside the amount needed for insurance deductibles in a savings or NOW checking account.

_____b. Begin building a savings account (preferably a money-market type which draws the highest interest) that will in time contain at least three months' salary.

_____c. Begin a savings plan from which you will eventually start investing.

_____ 5. Begin paying off existing debts.

_____ 6. Adjust daily, weekly, and monthly spending to reflect your budget plan (as completed in Appendix D).

_____ 7. If you do not already know the amount of your benefits from denominational pension and insurance programs and from social security, find out what they are.

_____ 8. Set up an adequate insurance program (life, disability, health care, and property) to guarantee that your goals will be achievable even in the event of death, disability, or lawsuit.

_____ 9. If eligible, set up a 403(b) retirement program and/or a Keogh plan.

_____10. Complete the Record of Insurance and Other Important Data (Appendix M).

_____11. Set up an I.R.A. for yourself and spouse.

_____12. If you liked the suggestion in chapter 12, begin purchasing food, household items, and routinely used goods in large discounted quantities.

_____13. Study investments, consult with financial advisor(s), and begin a program which will help you accomplish your goals as shown on your lifeline.

_____14. Continue to do whatever is necessary to help you achieve your dreams. (If necessary, revise the subgoals on your lifeline to adjust to changing circumstances and aspirations.)

Remember that you have to complete the worksheets on a regular basis. This material must be _used_ (not just read), if it is to help you with your financial affairs. It can also help you affirm that the Lord—not money—is number one in your life. Doing these exercises will show your priorities to yourself and others, by using your money constructively, rather than vice versa.

If you find yourself burdened with the process and becoming overconcerned with finances, review your lifeline, which should reveal your true feelings. Reaffirm to yourself that the worksheets are merely a technique to help you achieve certain goals in your lifetime.

14

A Last Word

As I mentioned earlier, a man once said, "Show me someone's checkbook and I'll tell you what that person thinks is important in life." Assuming that all your expenditures are recorded in your checkbook, a look at it can tell you how much you spend on food, clothes, shelter, entertainment, hobbies, charities, medical care, and everything else. The amount spent in each area is not necessarily all that you would consider, but expenses above and beyond the minimum for survival tell a lot about your priorities in life. We have talked about setting goals and managing money in order to reach them. But we have to be careful to keep those goals in mind and spend accordingly. For example, assume that you can live quite comfortably in a five-room house, yet you are making high payments on a ten-room house with a swimming pool. You may also be saying that you want something else, but "can't afford it." Obviously, you have set a higher priority on the larger home—no matter what you have been telling others and yourself. Look at your checkbook to see if your spending agrees in principle with your life's goals.

You start controlling your life through money management when you begin putting your money where your priorities are. If you think your church is important, some of your money should be going there. If you say good health is important, you should be spending money on a nutritiously balanced diet and perhaps join an exercise club. Don't be like the alcoholic who says he loves his family, yet spends all his money on liquor. "Put your money where your mouth is," to quote a fitting old expression!

But, you say, you already spend all the money that comes into the house on things that are necessary, or for prior obligations on other items. You may even claim that the sailboat in the back yard is part of your life plan (recreation *is* important) and that the payments on it would be the only flexible item in the budget. So how could you possibly spend money on other things you have said are also important? I believe that there is room to make some adjustments in any budget that is over a survival minimum. Maybe not right this minute, but within six months at a maximum, if you really mean what you say about your life planning. That does not mean that within a month or two you will be able to spend the entire amount projected for this area, but at least a little can be going in that direction.

Sit down and look carefully at your lifeline. For your most important goal, you have listed in order of priority the things you need to reach that aspiration. Then say, "If I could accomplish only one of the items on my plan, which would I pick?" Then do that with the second most important goal, and so on. What you are getting ready to do is determine how you can use some of your money *right now* (or at least soon) to work toward your ultimate aims. You will give or spend time in that area beginning right now!

Now ask yourself if your expenditures are reflective of what you say is important. Could anything be dropped? Could you do special things to demonstrate your value system with what you now have—such as selling your new sports car and buying an economy model? That way, you would not only eliminate the large payments, but would show that what you really want is transportation. That may not be practical in all cases, but something like that may be just what you need to do to show that you are really taking control of your life through how you spend your money.

Another way to reflect your priorities in your spending habits is to try to continue living at the same standard and put any extra money from raises and gifts into your new high-priority areas. Since there are many ways to change old habits and get into new ones, what I have suggested does not cover all the possibilities, only the most obvious ones.

There is a branch of psychology and counseling called "behavior modification." This approach tries to get people to change their unwanted habits by forcing themselves to behave in the fashion that they would like. At first this seems awkward and phony, a put-on, but when people practice the desired behavior long enough, it becomes a natural and regular part of their lifestyle. Remember, anything that is a habit now was once done in your past for the very first and second times. If you say you would really like to save money to go back to school, buy your own home, or whatever, you must begin saving *now,* no matter how little it has to be for the moment. Put the money in a savings account, just as if you were paying one of your regular monthly bills—and don't touch it. Have a different account for emergencies, but leave the savings-for-my-own-home account alone. If you do that for a while, it will get to be such a habit that you might even delay paying a bill, just to put money in that account. Add any extra money to that fund, too. Soon, instead of just oozing along without knowing where you are going or how you will get there, you will have developed attitudes and a lifestyle which will clearly demonstrate your priorities.

Some people think that using money to control life is wrong, arguing that "money is the root of all evil." Actually, that is a misquote from 1 Timothy 6:10 which says, "The love of money is the root of evil." In our modern world everyone has to deal with money. The trick is to use money—and not let it use you. I once met a man who had been seriously burned in an automobile accident and whose face looked terrible. He was a salesman. Someone asked if his looks affected his selling. He said it did, though not in the negative way that might be expected. He had gotten into sales as the fastest way to get enough money for plastic surgery and did not let his looks or even people's reactions to them get in the way of earning money for the surgery. He was not after money for its own sake, but for what it could do to help him accomplish his goal.

Act the way you want to be and you will be that way. Spend your money to reflect your values and goals in life, and you will see those goals accomplished and those values shown to the world by your life.

Appendix A
Projected Life's Earnings

If someone is twenty years old and has a church which this year pays $10,000 in salary and benefits (total cash salary, social security, insurance and retirement premiums paid by church on his or her behalf), and if he or she receives an increase in total salary and benefits of at least 5 percent per year until retirement at age sixty-five, here is what he or she will make each year (numbers are rounded to nearest dollar).

Age	Year of Employ-ment	Yearly Salary	Total To Date	Age	Year of Employ-ment	Yearly Salary	Total To Date
20	1	$10,000	$10,000	43	24	$30,720	$445,059
21	2	10,500	20,500	44	25	32,256	477,315
22	3	11,025	31,525	45	26	33,869	511,184
23	4	11,576	43,101	46	27	35,563	546,747
24	5	12,155	55,256	47	28	37,341	584,088
				48	29	39,208	623,296
25	6	12,763	68,019	49	30	41,168	664,464
26	7	13,401	81,420				
27	8	14,071	95,491	50	31	43,226	707,690
28	9	14,775	110,266	51	32	45,387	753,077
29	10	15,514	125,780	52	33	47,656	800,733
				53	34	50,039	850,772
30	11	16,290	142,070	54	35	52,541	903,313
31	12	17,105	159,175				
32	13	17,960	177,135	55	36	55,168	958,481
33	14	18,858	195,993	56	37	57,926	1,016,407
34	15	19,801	215,794	57	38	60,822	1,077,229
				58	39	63,863	1,141,092
35	16	20,791	236,585	59	40	67,056	1,208,148
36	17	21,831	258,416				
37	18	22,923	281,339	60	41	70,409	1,278,557
38	19	24,069	305,408	61	42	73,930	1,352,487
39	20	25,273	330,681	62	43	77,627	1,430,114
				63	44	81,508	1,511,622
40	21	26,537	357,218	64	45	85,583	1,597,205
41	22	27,864	385,082				
42	23	29,257	414,339				

At age sixty-five this person will retire, having had over $1,597,205 pass through his or her hands. If you would like to see how your future looks (with increases which average a minimum of 5 percent per year), just count down the chart to the number of years it is until you retire (second column) and find the figure which shows the total to date for that year (fourth column). Now multiply that figure by your current income divided by 10,000. (Example: if you make a $25,000 in total salary and benefits, divide that by 10,000 for a factor of 2.5. If you will retire in thirty years, look on the chart and find the corresponding figure of $664,464, which you now multiply by 2.5 for a total of $1,661,160.)

When counting your income, include the total of everything it costs the church to have you as pastor or employee (health insurance, pensions, and housing costs that are paid directly by the church), because if for some reason you had to quit working for the church, you would lose those benefits. They are part of your income, even if you do not receive them directly.

Where Are You Now?

ASSETS (What you have)
  Cash and cash-value items
    Checking Accounts and cash . . . .
    Savings Accounts (Passbook, C.D.'s) . . . . . .
    Cash Value of Insurance Policies . . . .
    Stocks, Bonds . . . .
    Other (Gold, Silver, Stamps, etc.) . . . .

  Other property
    Value of Auto(s) . . . .
    Value of Personal Items (clothing, etc.) . . . .
    Value of Furniture, Household Items . . . . . .
    Value of Home and Real Estate . . . .

  Miscellaneous Items of Worth

    _____ . . . .
    _____ . . . .
         Total Assets . . . .

LIABILITIES (What you owe)
    For Automobile(s) . . . .
    For Home/Real Estate (not rent) . . . .
    For Furniture, Household Items . . . .
    For Personal Items (such as charge cards)
    For Other Loans . . . .
    For Loans Against Cash Value of Insurance
    For Any Other Debt . . . .
         Total Liabilities . . . .

Net Worth (Assets Minus Liabilities) . . . .

INTANGIBLE WORTH (No *present* cash value, but of long-term value):
  Insurance
    Health/Hospitalization . . . . Yes ( ) No ( )
    Property (house, auto) . . . .   ( )   ( )
    Life (How much? _____)   ( )   ( )
    Disability (How much _____)   ( )   ( )
    Social Security (How many quarters paid?) _____   ( )   ( )
    Retirement, IRA Accounts, Etc. . . . .   ( )   ( )
    Other . . . .   ( )   ( )

Everyone has individual things of intangible worth that would not fit on this form, but you can think of those things for yourself. Even if your Net Worth is zero or a negative figure right now, a lot of intangibles might really offset that. But wherever you are, this is just the *starting* place.

Where Are You Going?

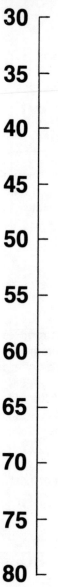

30

35

40

45

50

55

60

65

70

75

80

Illustrations follow on next pages. Also see chapter 3 for instructions, and Appendix N for sample strategies.

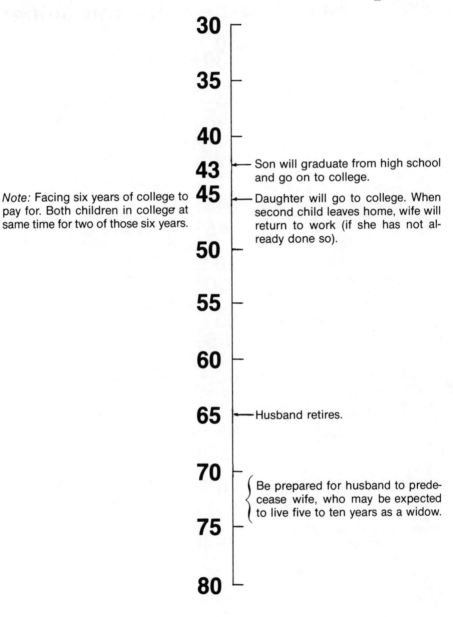

30

35

40

43 ◄—— Son will graduate from high school and go on to college.

Note: Facing six years of college to **45** ◄—— Daughter will go to college. When
pay for. Both children in college at second child leaves home, wife will
same time for two of those six years. return to work (if she has not already done so).

50

55

60

65 ◄—— Husband retires.

70
⎧ Be prepared for husband to prede-
⎨ cease wife, who may be expected
⎩ to live five to ten years as a widow.
75

80

95

Step Two
Major Goals

Step Three
Specific Plans

Begin doctoral studies

30

A A. Begin to manage life and money
to accomplish goals in Step Two:

35
    1. Get budget in order
    2. Begin savings program

B
    3. Buy a home
    4. Secure life insurance program

40
    5. Start making application for
       doctoral program

Finish doctoral program, so able
to assist children with college
expenses.

43
    6. Invest for future needs

45
B. Serve on denominational com-
mittees and boards to best show
talents with aim of being noticed by

C larger churches.

Be in a larger, urban church or be
a professor in a seminary.

50
C. Continue to invest and save to
help children and prepare for trav-
els later.

Be able to assist children with
homes or businesses. (Pay for
weddings?)

55

Have developed hobbies and begun
traveling—things that will be fun
both now and after retirement (perhaps travel in mission fields).

D D. Begin visiting members of con-
gregations who have interesting
60 hobbies, and start learning from
them.

65

Have paid for a car and a house
with which to start retirement years.

E E. Enjoy retirement and update estate planning.

70

Have managed financial planning so
that wife will be able to live comfortably until she dies.

75

80

Sample Monthly Budget Worksheets

The following two pages represent samples of how an imaginary couple might complete a monthly budget (Appendixes D-1 and D-2).

This young couple's total income is not particularly large, even though both are working. They are paying off some prior debt obligations and also saving for the husband to work on a doctoral program sometime in the future.

As explained in chapter 4, they have first prepared an *annual* budget (Table 1) and entered the appropriate amounts (adjusted budget) in the first column of Appendix D-1. Next they divided each annual appropriation by twelve to determine the monthly figures, which are entered in the second column.

At this point, they examine their monthly expenditures as reflected in their checkbook, and turn to Appendix D-2. They will enter all bills paid that month and any other expenditures which do not appear elsewhere. Remember, one check payment may actually represent more than one budget category. For example, a VISA payment may be allocated to Prior Debt Retirement, Auto Repairs, and Clothing. Individual charge slips should be retained for this purpose and also to verify the billing.

When all expenditures have been listed, the monthly total for each category is added to the Spent-this-Year figure from the worksheet for the *previous* month. The new yearly totals are then entered on the current monthly worksheet.

A careful study of expenditures may reveal apparent overspending or underspending in specific categories. For example, if all the insurance premiums come due at one time (perhaps annually), the budget entry for that month may show an overexpenditure, and an apparent underexpenditure will appear in the next several months. However, this is something which the couple would anticipate if they had a system to remind them of large upcoming bills. (If the annual amount is prorated for a monthly base, this should be no problem.) If food, medical, or other bills get out of hand, adjustments will have to be made in other categories for that month, or even for the next few months.

Sample Monthly Budget Worksheet

Month of March 198 2

Budget Category	Yearly Budget	Monthly Budget	Spent this Month	Spent this Year
Church/Charities	1800.00	150.00	150.00	450.00
Savings/Investments	1800.00	150.00	150.00	450.00
Food/Household Items	4800.00	400.00	347.18	1168.63
Clothing	1200.00	100.00	63.14	208.79
Housing: Mortgage/Rent	5400.00	450.00	450.00	1350.00
Utilities	2220.00	185.00	132.98	404.87
Furniture/Miscellaneous	1020.00	85.00	0	370.55
Transportation: Auto Payments	2340.00	195.00	195.00	585.00
Gas, Oil, Etc.	1500.00	125.00	92.78	332.06
Insurance	790.00	65.23	65.83	197.50
Repairs/Maintenance	600.00	50.00	14.82	383.71
Miscellaneous	60.00	5.00	47.03	47.03
Medical (doctor, dentist, medicine)	810.00	67.50	175.00	325.00
Personal Taxes (income/other)	2750.00	229.16	229.16	687.48
Insurance (life, health, other)	1512.00	126.00	0	586.00
Allowances/Personal Care	240.00	20.00	24.50	64.50
Entertainment (at home and away)	600.00	50.00	40.35	113.35
Celebrations (holidays, birthdays, anniversaries, etc.)	600.00	50.00	35.00	98.40
Rest/Relaxation (vacations, hobbies, recreation, etc.)	1200.00	100.00	68.00	173.04
Education/Enrichment (art/music lessons, books, etc.	900.00	75.00	54.00	287.12
Professional Expenses (tools, books, schools, not paid by employer)	450.00	37.50	120.00	120.00
Community Involvement (political parties, scouting, etc.)	300.00	25.00	0	0
Prior Debt Retirement	1020.00	85.00	85.00	255.00
Miscellaneous	900.00	75.00	118.47	216.90
TOTALS	34,812.00	2,900.99	2,623.24	8,875.13

Sample Monthly Expenditures

Month of __March__ 198 __2__

On Account With And/Or Budget Category		Previous Balance	Add/Subtract Charges, Credits, Interest, etc.	Pay this Month	New Balance
Church / Charities		0	150.00	150.00	0
Savings/ Investments	Money Market Fund	0	100.00	100.00	0
	Mutual Fund	0	25.00	25.00	0
	Payments on Rental Property and Repairs (Above what rental Income there is)	0	25.00	25.00	0
House	Payments	105,750		450.00	105,300
	Gas	0	58.84	58.84	0
	Electricity	0	47.89	47.89	0
	Water, Sewer, Garbage	0	14.75	14.75	0
	Telephone	0	11.50	11.50	0
Auto	Payments	3510.00			
	Repairs, Maintenance, Misc.	0	Trailer Hitch 47.03	47.03	0
	Insurance	658.34		65.83	592.51
Oil Credit Cards	Citco	0	0	0	0
	Conoco	0	67.80	67.80	0
	Gulf	0	13.75	13.75	0
	Mobil	0	11.23	11.23	0
	Tenneco	0	0	0	0
	Texaco	0	0	0	0
Insurance	Life	0	0	0	0
	Disability, Hospitalization	0	0	0	0
	Other	0	0	0	0
Dr. J. M. Brown		0	175.00	175.00	0
Personal Care		0	24.50	24.50	0
Entertainment (Cable TV)		0	15.95	15.95	0
Sears		0	0	0	0
Penny's (Prior Debt Retirement)*		+132.00	Service Charge + 1.25 *	20.00	113.25
VISA (Professional Books)*		+754.18	S.C. + 8.42 + 120.00 *	150.00	732.60
MasterCard (Children's Clothing)*		+803.11	S.C. + 9.06 + 63.14 *	98.14	777.17
Misc.	Music Lessons	0	42.50	42.50	0
	* (Both paid in full in addition to monthly minimum on previous balance)				
Total					

Appendix E
The Commissioners Standard Ordinary Mortality Table (1958 CSO)

Age	Number Living	Deaths Each Year	Death Rate per 1,000	Expectation of Life	Age	Number Living	Deaths Each Year	Death Rate per 1,000	Expectation of Life
0	10,000,000	70,800	7.08	68.30	50	8,762,306	72,902	8.32	23.63
1	9,929,200	17,475	1.76	67.78	51	8,689,404	79,160	9.11	22.82
2	9,911,725	15,066	1.52	66.90	52	8,610,244	85,758	9.96	22.03
3	9,896,659	14,449	1.46	66.00	53	8,524,486	92,832	10.89	21.25
4	9,882,210	13,835	1.40	65.10	54	8,431,654	100,337	11.90	20.47
5	9,868,375	13,322	1.35	64.19	55	8,331,317	108,307	13.00	19.71
6	9,855,053	12,812	1.30	63.27	56	8,223,010	116,849	14.21	18.97
7	9,842,241	12,401	1.26	62.35	57	8,106,161	125,970	15.54	18.23
8	9,829,840	12,091	1.23	61.43	58	7,980,191	135,663	17.00	17.51
9	9,817,749	11,879	1.21	60.51	59	7,844,528	145,830	18.59	16.81
10	9,805,870	11,865	1.21	59.58	60	7,698,698	156,592	20.34	16.12
11	9,794,005	12,047	1.23	58.65	61	7,542,106	167,736	22.24	15.44
12	9,781,958	12,325	1.26	57.72	62	7,374,370	179,271	24.31	14.78
13	9,769,633	12,896	1.32	56.80	63	7,195,099	191,174	26.57	14.14
14	9,756,737	13,562	1.39	55.87	64	7,003,925	203,394	29.04	13.51
15	9,743,175	14,225	1.46	54.95	65	6,800,531	215,917	31.75	12.90
16	9,728,950	14,983	1.54	54.03	66	6,584,614	228,749	34.74	12.31
17	9,713,967	15,737	1.62	53.11	67	6,355,865	241,777	38.04	11.73
18	9,698,230	16,390	1.69	52.19	68	6,114,088	254,835	41.68	11.17
19	9,681,840	16,846	1.74	51.28	69	5,859,253	267,241	45.61	10.64
20	9,664,994	17,300	1.79	50.37	70	5,592,012	278,426	49.79	10.12
21	9,647,694	17,655	1.83	49.46	71	5,313,586	287,731	54.15	9.63
22	9,630,039	17,912	1.86	48.55	72	5,025,855	294,766	58.65	9.15
23	9,612,127	18,167	1.89	47.64	73	4,731,089	299,289	63.26	8.69
24	9,593,960	18,324	1.91	46.73	74	4,431,800	301,894	68.12	8.24
25	9,575,636	18,481	1.93	45.82	75	4,129,906	303,011	73.37	7.81
26	9,557,155	18,732	1.96	44.90	76	3,826,895	303,014	79.18	7.39
27	9,538,423	18,981	1.99	43.99	77	3,523,881	301,997	85.70	6.98
28	9,519,442	19,324	2.03	43.08	78	3,221,884	299,829	93.06	6.59
29	9,500,118	19,760	2.08	42.16	79	2,922,055	295,683	101.19	6.21
30	9,480,358	20,193	2.13	41.25	80	2,626,372	288,848	109.98	5.85
31	9,460,165	20,718	2.19	40.34	81	2,337,524	278,983	119.35	5.51
32	9,439,447	21,239	2.25	39.43	82	2,058,541	265,902	129.17	5.19
33	9,418,208	21,850	2.32	38.51	83	1,792,639	249,858	139.38	4.89
34	9,396,358	22,551	2.40	37.60	84	1,542,781	231,433	150.01	4.60
35	9,373,807	23,528	2.51	36.69	85	1,311,348	211,311	161.14	4.32
36	9,350,279	24,685	2.64	35.78	86	1,100,037	190,108	172.82	4.06
37	9,325,594	26,112	2.80	34.88	87	909,929	168,455	185.13	3.80
38	9,299,482	27,991	3.01	33.97	88	741,474	146,997	198.25	3.55
39	9,271,491	30,132	3.25	33.07	89	594,477	126,303	212.46	3.31
40	9,241,359	32,622	3.53	32.18	90	468,174	106,809	228.14	3.06
41	9,208,737	35,362	3.84	31.29	91	361,365	88,813	245.77	2.82
42	9,173,375	38,253	4.17	30.41	92	272,552	72,480	265.93	2.58
43	9,135,122	41,382	4.53	29.54	93	200,072	57,881	289.30	2.33
44	9,093,740	44,741	4.92	28.67	94	142,191	45,026	316.66	2.07
45	9,048,999	48,412	5.35	27.81	95	97,165	34,128	351.24	1.80
46	9,000,587	53,473	5.83	26.95	96	63,037	25,250	400.56	1.51
47	8,948,114	56,910	6.36	26.11	97	37,787	18,456	488.42	1.18
48	8,891,204	61,794	6.95	25.27	98	19,331	12,916	668.15	.83
49	8,829,410	67,104	7.60	24.45	99	6,415	6,415	1,000.00	.50

Comparison Between Whole-Life and Term Insurance
Beginning Age 25

Age	(A) Annual Premium Investment	(B) Total Additions	(C) Total Cash Value	(D) Total Death Benefit	(E) Annual Renewable Term Premiums	(F) Difference To Invest	(G) Value of Investment	(H) Total Death Benefit
25	$1,020	0	0	$100,000	$190	$830	$880	$100,880
26	1,020	$321	$465	100,321	191	829	1,811	101,811
27	1,020	735	855	100,735	192	828	2,799	102,799
28	1,020	1,222	1,867	101,222	193	827	3,843	103,843
29	1,020	1,795	3,005	101,795	197	823	4,946	104,946
30	1,020	2,461	4,073	102,461	201	819	6,111	106,111
31	1,020	3,229	5,277	103,229	206	814	7,341	107,341
32	1,020	4,104	6,620	104,104	207	813	8,643	108,643
33	1,020	5,085	7,906	105,085	210	810	9,943	109,943
34	1,020	6,168	9,337	106,168	214	806	11,393	111,393
35	1,020	7,357	10,917	107,357	221	799	12,924	112,924
36	1,020	8,654	12,552	108,654	230	790	14,536	114,536
37	1,020	10,059	14,244	110,059	242	778	16,233	116,233
38	1,020	11,579	16,100	111,579	255	765	18,018	118,018
39	1,020	13,215	18,025	113,215	271	749	19,893	119,893
40	1,020	14,953	20,018	114,953	291	729	21,860	121,860
41	1,020	16,800	22,087	116,800	309	711	23,925	123,925
42	1,020	18,759	24,336	118,758	331	689	26,091	126,091
43	1,020	20,828	26,671	120,828	355	665	28,361	128,361
44	1,020	23,005	29,196	123,005	383	637	30,738	130,738
64	1,000	95,349	111,144	195,349	2,154	−1,154	103,117	203,117

Dividends are paid at the end of the second year. For the whole-life policy, they are used to purchase paid-up additions. For the term policy, they are used to reduce the next year's premium, to produce the figure in column (E).

Columns (B), (C), (D), (G), and (H), are end-of-year figures, while columns (A), (E), and (F), are beginning-of-the-year figures.

Column (G) is the value of investments as a net total less taxes and if ART (annual renewable term) premiums show a negative investment amount, that is deducted at the first of the year from investment total before increases. The figures in column (G) are the net value of an 8% net increase for a 25% tax bracket or 10% net increase for a 40% tax bracket or a 12% net increase for a 50% tax bracket.

Comparison Between Whole-Life and Term Insurance
Beginning Age 30

Age	(A) Annual Premium Investment	(B) Total Additions	(C) Total Cash Value	(D) Total Death Benefit	(E) Annual Renewable Term Premiums	(F) Difference To Invest	(G) Value of Investment	(H) Total Death Benefit
30	$1,247	0	0	$100,000	$ 201	$1,046	$ 1,109	$101,109
31	1,247	$ 261	$ 562	100,261	206	1,041	2,279	102,279
32	1,247	617	1,053	100,617	207	1,040	3,523	103,523
33	1,247	1,070	2,275	101,070	210	1,037	4,834	104,834
34	1,247	1,613	3,628	101,613	214	1,033	6,219	106,219
35	1,247	2,276	5,024	102,276	221	1,026	7,680	107,680
36	1,247	3,056	6,465	103,056	230	1,017	8,703	108,703
37	1,247	3,953	8,057	103,953	242	1,005	10,290	110,290
38	1,247	4,976	9,704	104,976	255	992	11,959	111,959
39	1,247	6,123	11,511	106,123	271	976	13,712	113,712
40	1,247	7,394	13,382	107,394	291	956	15,548	115,548
41	1,247	8,797	15,325	108,797	309	938	17,475	117,475
42	1,247	10,329	17,344	110,329	331	916	19,494	119,494
43	1,247	11,991	19,544	111,991	355	892	21,609	121,609
44	1,247	13,780	21,829	113,780	383	864	23,822	123,822
45	1,247	15,682	24,300	115,682	412	835	26,136	126,136
46	1,247	17,705	26,764	117,705	445	802	28,554	128,554
47	1,247	19,846	29,426	119,846	482	765	31,079	131,079
48	1,247	22,108	32,292	122,108	527	720	33,706	133,706
49	1,247	24,488	35,266	124,488	578	669	36,438	136,438
64	1,220	77,724	98,067	177,724	2,154	–934	89,747	189,747

Dividends are paid at the end of the second year. For the whole-life policy, they are used to purchase paid-up additions. For the term policy, they are used to reduce the next year's premium, to produce the figure in column (E).

Columns (B), (C), (D), (G), and (H), are end-of-year figures, while columns (A), (E), and (F), are beginning-of-the-year figures.

Column (G) is the value of investments as a net total less taxes and if ART (annual renewable term) premiums show a negative investment amount, that is deducted at the first of the year from investment total before increases. The figures in column (G) are the net value of an 8% net increase for a 25% tax bracket or 10% net increase for a 40% tax bracket or a 12% net increase for a 50% tax bracket.

Appendix F-3
Comparison Between Whole-Life and Term Insurance
Beginning Age 35

Age	(A) Annual Premium Investment	(B) Total Additions	(C) Total Cash Value	(D) Total Death Benefit	(E) Annual Renewable Term Premiums	(F) Difference To Invest	(G) Value of Investment	(H) Total Death Benefit
35	$1,550	0	0	$100,000	$ 221	$1,329	$ 1,409	$101,409
36	1,550	$ 254	$ 671	100,254	230	1,320	2,893	102,893
37	1,550	614	1,380	100,614	242	1,308	4,463	104,463
38	1,550	1,091	2,929	101,091	255	1,295	6,103	106,103
39	1,550	1,682	4,525	101,682	271	1,279	7,825	107,825
40	1,550	2,414	6,278	102,414	291	1,259	9,629	109,629
41	1,550	3,286	8,092	103,286	309	1,241	11,522	111,522
42	1,550	4,301	9,975	104,301	331	1,219	13,506	113,506
43	1,550	5,454	11,930	105,454	355	1,195	15,583	115,583
44	1,550	6,745	14,061	106,745	383	1,167	17,755	117,755
45	1,550	8,171	16,374	108,171	412	1,138	20,026	120,026
46	1,550	9,741	18,676	109,741	445	1,105	22,399	122,399
47	1,550	11,453	21,174	111,453	482	1,068	24,875	124,875
48	1,550	13,304	23,771	113,304	527	1,023	27,452	127,452
49	1,550	15,291	26,573	115,291	578	972	30,130	130,130
50	1,550	17,402	29,480	117,402	638	912	32,904	132,904
51	1,550	19,644	32,500	119,644	696	854	35,783	135,783
52	1,550	22,027	35,644	122,027	761	789	38,767	138,767
53	1,550	24,553	39,019	124,553	822	728	41,865	141,865
54	1,550	27,222	42,430	127,222	897	653	45,069	145,069
64	1,511	62,429	85,827	162,429	2,154	−643	82,027	182,027

Dividends are paid at the end of the second year. For the whole-life policy, they are used to purchase paid-up additions. For the term policy, they are used to reduce the next year's premium, to produce the figure in column (E).

Columns (B), (C), (D), (G), and (H) are end-of-year figures, while columns (A), (E), and (F), are beginning-of-the-year figures.

Column (G) is the value of investments as a net total less taxes and if ART (annual renewable term) premiums show a negative investment amount, that is deducted at the first of the year from investment total before increases. The figures in column (G) are the net value of an 8% net increase for a 25% tax bracket or 10% net increase for a 40% tax bracket or a 12% net increase for a 50% tax bracket.

Comparison Between Whole-Life and Term Insurance
Beginning Age 40

Age	(A) Annual Premium Investment	(B) Total Additions	(C) Total Cash Value	(D) Total Death Benefit	(E) Annual Renewable Term Premiums	(F) Difference To Invest	(G) Value of Investment	(H) Total Death Benefit
40	$1,950	0	0	$100,000	$ 291	$1,659	$ 1,759	$101,759
41	1,950	$ 327	$ 908	100,327	309	1,641	3,605	103,605
42	1,950	786	1,869	100,786	331	1,619	5,556	105,556
43	1,950	1,375	3,786	101,375	355	1,595	7,580	107,580
44	1,950	2,091	5,763	102,091	383	1,567	9,696	109,696
45	1,950	2,957	7,812	102,957	412	1,538	11,908	111,908
46	1,950	3,979	10,042	103,979	445	1,505	14,218	114,218
47	1,950	5,155	12,359	105,155	482	1,468	16,627	116,627
48	1,950	6,483	14,766	106,483	527	1,423	19,133	119,133
49	1,950	7,962	17,370	107,962	578	1,372	21,735	121,735
50	1,950	9,588	19,976	109,588	638	1,312	24,430	124,430
51	1,950	11,371	22,894	111,371	696	1,254	27,225	127,225
52	1,950	13,319	25,834	113,319	761	1,189	30,119	130,119
53	1,950	15,431	29,002	115,431	822	1,128	33,122	133,122
54	1,950	17,708	32,306	117,708	897	1,053	36,225	136,225
55	1,950	20,125	35,741	120,125	986	964	39,421	139,421
56	1,950	22,681	39,312	122,681	1,093	857	42,694	142,694
57	1,950	25,378	43,025	125,378	1,207	743	46,043	146,043
58	1,950	28,227	46,992	128,227	1,329	621	49,464	149,464
59	1,950	31,236	51,124	131,236	1,455	495	52,957	152,957
64	1,894	48,988	73,832	148,988	2,154	−260	71,677	171,677

Dividends are paid at the end of the second year. For the whole-life policy, they are used to purchase paid-up additions. For the term policy, they are used to reduce the next year's premium, to produce the figure in column (E).

Columns (B), (C), (D), (G), and (H), are end-of-year figures, while columns (A), (E), and (F), are beginning-of-the-year figures.

Column (G) is the value of investments as a net total less taxes and if ART (annual renewable term) premiums show a negative investment amount, that is deducted at the first of the year from investment total before increases. The figures in column (G) are the net value of an 8% net increase for a 25% tax bracket or a 10% net increase for a 40% tax bracket or a 12% net increase for a 50% tax bracket.

Comparison Between Whole-Life and Term Insurance
Beginning Age 45

Age	(A) Annual Premium Investment	(B) Total Additions	(C) Total Cash Value	(D) Total Death Benefit	(E) Annual Renewable Term Premiums	(F) Difference To Invest	(G) Value of Investment	(H) Total Death Benefit
45	$2,484	0	0	$100,000	$ 412	$2,072	$ 2,196	$102,196
46	2,484	$ 459	$ 1,277	100,459	445	2,039	4,391	104,391
47	2,484	1,060	2,623	101,060	482	2,002	6,812	106,812
48	2,484	1,804	4,942	101,804	527	1,957	9,295	109,295
49	2,484	2,687	7,337	102,687	578	1,906	11,873	111,873
50	2,484	3,733	9,826	103,733	638	1,846	14,542	114,542
51	2,484	4,953	12,419	104,953	696	1,788	17,310	117,310
52	2,484	6,348	15,223	106,348	761	1,723	20,175	120,175
53	2,484	7,924	18,149	107,924	822	1,662	23,147	123,147
54	2,484	9,677	21,303	109,677	897	1,587	26,218	126,218
55	2,484	11,598	24,486	111,598	986	1,498	29,379	129,379
56	2,484	13,685	27,906	113,685	1,093	1,391	32,616	132,616
57	2,484	15,941	31,470	115,941	1,207	1,277	35,927	135,927
58	2,484	18,374	35,189	118,374	1,329	1,155	39,307	139,307
59	2,484	20,992	39,075	120,992	1,455	1,029	42,756	142,756
60	2,395	23,788	43,231	123,788	1,451	944	46,322	146,322
61	2,395	26,767	47,466	126,767	1,594	801	49,950	149,950
62	2,395	29,932	51,889	129,932	1,754	641	53,627	153,627
63	2,395	33,278	56,503	133,278	1,942	453	57,324	157,324
64	2,395	36,807	61,415	136,807	2,154	241	61,019	161,019

Dividends are paid at the end of the second year. For the whole-life policy, they are used to purchase paid-up additions. For the term policy, they are used to reduce the next year's premium, to produce the figure in column (E).

Columns (B), (C), (D), (G), and (H), are end-of-year figures, while columns (A), (E), and (F), are beginning-of-the-year figures.

Column (G) is the value of investments as a net total less taxes and if ART (annual renewable term) premiums show a negative investment amount, that is deducted at the first of the year from investment total before increases. The figures in column (G) are the net value of an 8% net increase for a 25% tax bracket or 10% net increase for a 40% tax bracket or a 12% net increase for a 50% tax bracket.

Depletion/Preservation of an Estate

There are different ways of dealing with the capital in an estate, or with the money that one has at the beginning of retirement. The charts which follow show various alternative methods of using and/or preserving capital, and the time it takes to deplete an estate if that is what is desired. Since it is impossible to account for every possible variation in interest and inflation rates, the charts use representative rates to give a general idea. The sample capital base is $100,000. If your estate or retirement fund has more, just multiply everything by the factor of your estate value over that figure (e.g., if your retirement fund or estate had $456,784 you would multiply everything by 4.45784).

Figure G-1

	Capital at Beginning of Year	Less Amount Withdrawn First of Each Year	Rate of Return on Investments	Number of Years Until Estate is Totally Depleted
A.	$100,000	$15,000	10%	9.78
B.	100,000	10,000	10%	25.17

If you wish to take inflation into account for your living expenses, you can increase what you withdraw each year. The following three items show how long it would take to deplete an estate if the initial withdrawal is $10,000 and each year increased by 5% in C, 7.5% in D, and 10% in E.

C.	$100,000	$10,000 + 5% annual increase	10%	13.10
D.	100,000	10,000 + 7.5% annual increase	10%	11.48
E.	100,000	10,000 + 10% annual increase	10%	10.00

As you can see, a flat withdrawal rate can last from almost ten years to a little over twenty-five years, but the problem is that it costs more to live each year—so the amount withdrawn would not purchase as much as the year before. If you increase the amount withdrawn, that decreases the number of years the estate or retirement fund will last.

An alternative is to start with a larger estate (capital base), live off less than the total investment return and reinvest part of the return each year so that the capital base keeps growing, allowing you to have more each year on which to live.

Figure G-2

Capital Base	Less 5%	Difference To Invest	10% Increase	Capital Base At End of Year	Year #
$200,000	$10,000	$190,000	$19,000	$209,000	1
209,000	10,450	198,550	19,855	218,405	2
218,405	10,920	207,485	20,749	228,234	3
238,504	11,925	226,579	22,658	249,237	5
297,219	14,861	282,358	28,236	310,594	10
370,388	18,519	351,869	35,187	387,056	15

And so on indefinitely. I doubled the original capital base just so the amount withdrawn would be $10,000. You could work with any figure so long as the principle followed was that you reinvested each year so that you lived on less than the capital base earned in income. In theory, in times of high inflation (when you would need more on which to live), you would be getting more return on the investments, so you could take more out of the pot for living expenses.

There may be reasons that one might not wish to leave an estate (such as trying to avoid estate taxes), so the following chart shows how much can be withdrawn from a beginning account of $100,000 at various percentages of investment return for years five through thirty. The assumption is that equal amounts are withdrawn the first of each year and the person lives on that amount during the year, while the remainder draws the interest at the top of the column. Numbers have been rounded to the nearest five-dollar figure. At the end of the number of years for which you wish to work, there will be a few dollars left, but in every case it is less than one-twelfth of an annual withdrawal.

If your estate is higher or lower, just adjust the figures by the factor that your estate exceeds $100,000 or is less than that (example: a $200,000 estate would allow twice the withdrawal; or a $50,000 estate would only allow half the withdrawal).

Figure G-3

Years	6%	8%	10%	12%	14%	16%
5	$22,395	$23,185	$23,975	$24,755	$25,550	$26,325
10	12,800	13,775	14,750	15,800	16,800	17,800
15	9,700	10,815	11,950	13,105	14,280	15,460
20	8,225	9,425	10,675	11,950	13,240	14,540
25	7,375	8,680	10,010	11,380	12,760	14,135
30	6,850	8,220	9,640	11,085	12,525	13,955

There are two immediate situations which might apply to this chart. One is that you may have move in with you a person such as a parent who has his or her own estate. If that person wanted to give you gifts of money (current nontaxable limit at the writing of this book is $10,000 per year) that would reduce the estate on which taxes would have to be paid, you can see how many years it would take to use up the estate with such gifts.

Another use it to dispel the idea that your own estate would provide a great income for years to come, even if you do not use the technique of investment which is explained in Figure G-2.

Taxes and Housing

For income tax purposes, ministers for many years have been able to deduct both property taxes and interest paid on their own home—and also did not have to report their housing allowance as taxable income, so long as they used the entire allowance for housing. On January 3, 1983, however, the IRS issued a new ruling which somewhat changed that. Now you are still not required to report the housing allowance as taxable income, but you may deduct only a portion of the interest and taxes on your home. If you wish to check this with your tax advisor, it is covered in IRS Rev. Rul 83-3. Below is an illustration of how this now applies.

During the taxable year, a minister received $20,000 in cash salary from his congregation and $9,600 for a housing allowance and utilities. During the year his housing expenses were:

Principal on loan payments	$ 350
Insurance	500
Real estate taxes	1,450
Interest on loan	6,150
Utilities	2,600
Total	$11,050

Under the old system, the minister could deduct both the interest ($6,150) and the taxes ($1,450) to the full amount paid. Under the new ruling, the minister must multiply the items that he or she wishes to deduct by a figure determined by dividing the amount of the housing allowance by the total cost of running the home. The result of the multiplication is subtracted from the original item to arrive at the allowable amount which can be deducted.

Interest

$6,150 × $\dfrac{\$9,600 \text{ (housing allowance)}}{11,050 \text{ (total housing expenses)}}$ = $5,443

Allowable deduction for interest:

$6,150
− 5,443
$ 707

Real estate taxes

$1,450 × $\dfrac{\$9,600 \text{ (housing allowance)}}{11,050 \text{ (total housing expenses)}}$ = $1,260

Allowable deduction for real estate taxes:

$1,450
− 1,260
$ 190

A later interpretation, IRS Announcement 83-100 has modified the effective date of Rev. Rul 83-3 for some persons. It states that if a minister owned and occupied a home before January 3, 1983, or had a contract to purchase a home before that date and then owns and occupies it, this ruling does not take effect until the minister moves out of the home or until January 1, 1985, whichever comes first. For those who purchase a home after January 3, 1983, the ruling is now in effect and will be in effect for everyone after January 1, 1985.

Return on Investments
Based on Investing $1,000 each January 1

Year #	Rate of Return Percentage					
	6%	8%	10%	12%	14%	16%
1	$ 1,060	$ 1,080	$ 1,100	$ 1,120	$ 1,140	$ 1,160
2	2,184	2,246	2,310	2,374	2,440	2,505
3	3,375	3,506	3,641	3,779	3,922	4,067
4	4,637	4,866	5,105	5,352	5,611	5,878
5	5,975	6,335	6,716	7,114	7,537	7,978
6	7,394	7,922	8,488	9,088	9,732	10,414
7	8,897	9,636	10,437	11,299	12,234	13,240
8	10,491	11,487	12,581	13,775	15,087	16,518
9	12,181	13,486	14,939	16,548	18,339	20,321
10	13,972	15,645	17,533	19,654	22,046	24,732
11	15,870	17,977	20,386	23,132	26,272	29,849
12	17,882	20,495	23,525	27,028	31,090	35,785
13	20,015	23,215	26,978	31,391	36,583	42,671
14	22,276	26,152	30,776	36,278	42,845	50,658
15	24,672	29,324	34,954	41,751	49,983	59,923
16	27,213	32,750	39,548	47,881	58,121	70,671
17	29,906	36,450	44,603	54,747	67,398	83,138
18	32,760	40,446	50,163	62,437	77,974	97,600
19	35,786	44,762	56,280	71,049	90,030	114,376
20	38,993	49,423	63,008	80,695	103,774	133,836
21	42,392	54,457	70,409	91,498	119,442	156,410
22	45,996	59,894	78,550	103,598	137,304	182,596
23	49,816	65,766	87,505	117,150	157,667	212,971
24	53,864	72,107	97,356	132,328	180,880	248,206
25	58,156	78,956	108,192	149,327	207,343	289,079
26	62,705	86,352	120,111	163,430	237,511	336,492
27	67,527	94,340	133,222	184,162	271,903	391,491
28	72,639	102,967	147,644	207,381	311,109	455,290
29	78,057	112,284	163,508	233,387	355,804	529,296
30	83,800	122,347	179,959	262,513	406,757	615,143
31	89,888	132,215	199,055	295,135	464,843	714,726
32	96,341	144,952	220,061	331,672	531,061	830,242
33	103,181	157,628	243,167	372,593	606,550	964,241
34	110,432	171,318	268,584	418,424	692,607	1,119,680
35	118,118	186,103	296,542	469,755	790,712	1,299,989
36	126,265	202,071	327,296	527,246	902,552	1,509,147
37	134,901	219,317	361,126	591,636	1,030,049	1,751,771
38	144,055	237,942	398,339	663,752	1,175,396	2,033,214
39	153,758	258,057	439,273	744,522	1,341,361	2,359,688
40	164,043	279,782	484,300	834,985	1,530,292	2,738,398
41	174,946	303,245	533,830	936,303	1,745,673	3,177,702
42	186,503	328,585	588,313	1,049,779	1,991,207	3,687,294
43	198,753	355,952	648,244	1,176,872	2,271,116	4,278,421
44	211,738	385,508	714,168	1,319,217	2,590,212	4,964,128
45	225,502	417,429	786,685	1,478,643	2,953,982	5,759,548

Numbers have been rounded to the nearest dollar and are to be considered estimates, not precise tabulations. Below are two examples of how to use the charts.

Example 1: You begin an investment program in something like an annuity which is then paying 12% and put money into the program for six years, at which time the company changes the interest rate to 10%. Then you place your deposits in the annuity for another three years before the rate is dropped to 8%, at which it remains until you withdraw your money fifteen years later. How much is your investment worth?

First move six years down the 12% column and find the number $9,088. Move to the 10% column and find the figure closest to $9,088, which is $8,488. From that point, move down the 10% column three years to $14,939. Since the interest rate now changes to 8%, you move to the 8% column to find the figure closest to $14,939, which is $15,645. Now move down from there fifteen years to get a final figure of $78,956. Although this is a very rough estimate, it will give you a general idea of wht an annual investment of $1,000 would yield during times of varying interest rates.

Example 2: You invest ten years at 16%, then five years at 6%, seven years at 14%, and finally eight years at 8%. What will your investment be worth?

First go down the 16% column ten years and find $24,732. Now move to the 6% column to find the nearest figure to $24,732, which is $24,672. From that point, go down the 6% column five years to the figure $38,993. Again move to another column, 14%, where the nearest number to $38,993 is $36,583. Count down from there seven years to find $103,774. Going back to the 8% column, we find the nearest number to that is $102,967. Eight years down from that point locates a rough total of $202,071.

Remember, after the first time, forget the year numbers at the side of the table. Just count down the column from the figure you have located as nearest the one you previously found. In the second example, we actually invested for thirty years, but ended up on the thirty-six-year line of the 8% column.

Retirement Annuity Illustrations

If you had $1,200 per year to put into an annuity—and that is *all* you wanted to do—you could use the chart in Appendix I, Return on Investments, to see how much the investment would be worth at age sixty-five. For example, a thirty-year-old would look at the column showing a specified percentage of return and multiply the number shown for the thirty-fifth year of investing by 1.2 (the ratio of the actual investment of $1,200 to the base of $1,000 used in the table). Thus: $296,542 x 1.2 = $355,850.

The only problem with this type of investment is that if you die in the early years, there is a relatively small return from the investment. A way to build up an annuity and also guarantee a reasonable return for survivors is to combine the annuity program with an insurance policy (the least expensive decreasing term) with, in our illustrations, a death benefit of $100,000.

As you can see from Appendix J-2, a thirty-year-old with such an arrangement would have a total death benefit for his or her beneficiaries which would never be less than $73,000, even though the annuity value at the time (at age forty-three) is only $30,745. Also, by age fifty-four, since the annuity is valued at over $100,000, the insurance policy can be dropped altogether and the entire $1,200 be put into the annuity from then on. The resulting value at age sixty-five is lower than if all the money had been placed annually in the annuity, but there is an element of protection which would not be present in the annuity program alone.

There are five tables provided for various ages (J-1 to J-5). Each of the illustrations uses an insurance protection benefit of $100,000. The difference between the annual premium for the policy and $1,200 is invested in the annuity. The death benefit for a given year is the annuity value at the end of the previous year plus the insurance benefit plus the amount invested for that year. Again look at the thirty-year-old's table to discover that at age forty, the death benefit would be the insurance benefit ($58,089) plus the annuity value at the end of age thirty-nine ($17,515) plus the investment for the current year ($999)—for a total of $76,603.

Annuity/Insurance Program
Annual Cost of $1,200
Beginning at Age 25

Age	Insurance Death Benefit	Net Premium	Deposit In Annuity	End-of-Year Annuity Value (at 10%)	Total Death Benefit During Year
25	$100,000	$190	$1,010	$ 1,111	$101,010
26	100,000	191	1,009	2,333	102,120
27	100,000	192	1,008	3,675	103,341
28	100,000	193	1,007	5,150	104,682
29	100,000	197	1,003	6,768	106,153
30	100,000	201	999	8,544	107,767
31	90,286	201	999	10,497	99,829
32	89,265	201	999	12,646	100,761
33	87,293	201	999	15,000	100,938
34	84,946	201	999	17,599	100,945
35	81,865	201	999	20,458	100,463
36	77,832	201	999	23,603	99,289
37	73,148	201	999	27,062	97,750
38	68,103	201	999	30,867	96,164
39	63,200	201	999	35,053	95,066
40	58,089	201	999	39,657	94,141
41	53,742	201	999	44,622	94,398
42	49,686	201	999	50,183	95,307
43	45,798	201	999	56,300	96,980
44	42,134	201	999	63,029	99,433
45	38,726	201	999	70,431	102,754
46	35,586	201	999	78,573	107,016
47	32,578	201	999	87,529	112,150
48	29,644	201	999	97,381	118,172
49	0	0	1,200	108,439	98,581
50	0	0	1,200	120,603	109,639
55	0	0	1,200	202,291	183,901
60	0	0	1,200	333,850	303,500
61	0	0	1,200	368,556	335,050
62	0	0	1,200	406,731	369,756
63	0	0	1,200	448,724	407,931
64	0	0	1,200	494,917	449,924

Annuity/Insurance Program
Annual Cost of $1,200
Beginning at Age 30

Age	Insurance Death Benefit	Net Premium	Deposit In Annuity	End-of-Year Annuity Value (at 10%)	Total Death Benefit During Year
30	$100,000	$201	$ 999	$ 1,099	$100,999
31	90,286	201	999	2,308	92,384
32	89,265	201	999	3,637	92,572
33	87,293	201	999	5,100	91,929
34	84,946	201	999	6,709	91,045
35	81,865	201	999	8,480	89,573
36	77,832	201	999	10,427	87,311
37	73,148	201	999	12,568	84,574
38	68,108	201	999	14,924	81,675
39	63,200	201	999	17,515	79,123
40	58,089	201	999	20,366	76,603
41	53,742	201	999	23,501	75,107
42	49,686	201	999	26,951	74,186
43	45,798	201	999	30,745	73,748
44	42,134	201	999	34,919	73,878
45	38,726	201	999	39,508	74,644
46	35,586	201	999	44,558	76,093
47	32,578	201	999	50,113	78,135
48	29,644	201	999	56,224	80,756
49	26,825	201	999	62,945	84,048
50	24,196	201	999	70,339	88,140
51	22,036	201	999	78,471	93,374
52	20,257	201	999	87,418	99,727
53	18,589	201	999	97,259	107,006
54	0	0	1,200	108,305	98,459
55	0	0	1,200	120,455	109,505
56	0	0	1,200	133,821	121,655
57	0	0	1,200	148,523	135,021
58	0	0	1,200	164,695	149,723
59	0	0	1,200	182,485	165,895
60	0	0	1,200	202,053	183,685
61	0	0	1,200	223,579	203,253
62	0	0	1,200	247,257	224,779
63	0	0	1,200	273,302	248,457
64	0	0	1,200	301,952	274,502

Annuity/Insurance Program
Annual Cost of $1,200
Beginning at Age 35

Age	Insurance Death Benefit	Net Premium	Deposit In Annuity	End-of-Year Annuity Value (at 10%)	Total Death Benefit During Year
35	$100,000	$221	$ 979	$ 1,077	$100,979
36	86,699	221	979	2,261	88,755
37	81,481	221	979	3,565	84,721
38	75,861	221	979	4,998	80,405
39	70,400	221	979	6,575	76,377
40	64,706	221	979	8,310	72,260
41	59,865	221	979	10,218	69,154
42	55,347	221	979	12,318	66,544
43	51,015	221	979	14,625	64,312
44	46,934	221	979	17,165	62,538
45	43,138	221	979	19,958	61,282
46	39,640	221	979	23,031	60,577
47	36,289	221	979	26,411	60,299
48	33,021	221	979	30,130	60,411
49	29,881	221	979	34,220	60,990
50	26,953	221	979	38,717	62,152
51	24,547	221	979	43,666	64,243
52	22,565	221	979	49,110	67,210
53	20,706	221	979	55,098	70,795
54	18,966	221	979	61,685	75,043
55	17,222	221	979	68,930	79,886
56	15,562	221	979	76,900	85,471
57	14,069	221	979	85,667	91,948
58	12,781	221	979	95,312	99,427
59	0	0	1,200	106,163	96,512
60	0	0	1,200	118,099	107,363
61	0	0	1,200	131,229	119,299
62	0	0	1,200	145,672	132,429
63	0	0	1,200	161,560	146,872
64	0	0	1,200	179,036	162,760

Annuity/Insurance Program
Annual Cost of $1,200
Beginning at Age 40

Age	Insurance Death Benefit	Net Premium	Deposit In Annuity	End-of-Year Annuity Value (at 10%)	Total Death Benefit During Year
40	$100,000	$291	$909	$ 1,000	$100,909
41	82,654	291	909	2,100	84,563
42	76,416	291	909	3,310	79,425
43	70,436	291	909	4,640	74,655
44	64,801	291	909	6,105	70,350
45	59,559	291	909	7,716	66,573
46	54,731	291	909	9,487	63,356
47	50,104	291	909	11,436	60,500
48	45,592	291	909	13,580	57,937
49	41,257	291	909	15,937	55,746
50	37,213	291	909	18,531	54,059
51	33,891	291	909	21,384	53,331
52	31,155	291	909	24,523	53,448
53	28,589	291	909	27,975	54,021
54	26,186	291	909	31,773	55,070
55	23,778	291	909	35,949	56,460
56	21,486	291	909	40,544	58,344
57	19,425	291	909	45,598	60,878
58	17,647	291	909	51,158	64,154
59	16,113	291	909	57,274	68,180
60	14,799	291	909	64,002	72,982
61	13,455	291	909	71,402	78,366
62	12,218	291	909	79,542	84,529
63	11,035	291	909	88,497	91,486
64	9,946	291	909	98,347	99,352

Annuity/Insurance Program
Annual Cost of $1,200
Beginning at Age 45

Age	Insurance Death Benefit	Net Premium	Deposit In Annuity	End-of-Year Annuity Value (at 10%)	Total Death Benefit During Year
45	$100,000	$412	$788	$ 867	$100,788
46	80,858	412	788	1,820	82,513
47	74,022	412	788	2,869	76,630
48	67,356	412	788	4,023	71,013
49	60,951	412	788	5,292	65,762
50	54,977	412	788	6,689	61,057
51	50,069	412	788	8,224	57,546
52	46,027	412	788	9,914	55,039
53	42,236	412	788	11,722	52,938
54	38,686	412	788	13,816	51,246
55	35,128	412	788	16,064	49,732
56	31,743	412	788	18,538	48,595
57	28,698	412	788	21,259	48,024
58	26,071	412	788	24,251	48,118
59	23,805	412	788	27,544	48,844
60	21,863	412	788	31,164	50,195
61	19,878	412	788	35,147	51,830
62	18,051	412	788	39,528	53,986
63	16,302	412	788	44,349	56,618
64	14,694	412	788	49,650	59,831

A Plan for Estate Distribution

This plan is to allow a person to live comfortably in retirement, yet pass on to heirs the maximum amount of estate with little or no federal estate taxes due. The size of a "taxable estate" increases each year until 1987, so we will assume that this plan applies to someone who will die after 1987. While the exemption covers an estate of $600,000, one does not have to have an estate that large to need this plan, as a good investment program will make a much smaller estate reach that size, even in retirement.

For an example, we will assume a husband and wife who have assets at his age sixty-five that total $500,000. With inflation and a good investment program, more and more people are going to be in this situation. There are two sources of income during retirement that many people will have: Social security and an employer pension plan. Since everyone will not have an employer pension plan and those that do will vary so much, we will not take that into account in this illustration. If you have such a pension, and you decide to use this plan, then the pension can be used to buy extra things (gifts for grandchildren, trips around the world, and so on). We will assume a monthly social security benefit of $600, or $7,200 per year.

There are a few other assumptions and facts that are used in this illustration. Current regulations allow up to $10,000 per year to be given each year to someone else, income-tax-free to the receiver. The $10,000 gift has to be from money the giver has already paid income tax on, as the gifts are intended to reduce estate taxes. If the gift is given within the three years immediately prior to the giver's death, the gift is still calculated in the giver's estate tax even though the receiver has the money. For our illustration, we will assume four heirs who may receive up to $10,000 yearly from the estate owners (if both husband and wife own the estate, they could jointly give $20,000 to each heir, so the illustration can be adjusted accordingly, but we will assume a total of $40,000 per year given as gifts.)

Inflation has averaged about 7 percent per year over the last twenty years. A good investment program should be able to return at least 10 percent when inflation is 7 percent, so we will use those two numbers in our illustration, as an average (even though we know both will go up and down over the years). We will assume that our retired person(s) can live comfortably on $25,000 this year. Deducting the $7,200 from social security, that means he or she must use $17,800 from the estate. That is fine for this year, and we need to keep the same level of purchasing ability each year in the future. We will assume that social security will adjust according to inflation, so we need to increase our retired person's yearly allowance by 7 percent per year to keep up with inflation. Thus the $17,800 will increase each year until the person dies at age eighty. Again, people may die sooner or later, but our illustration is for the age by which over 70 percent of all people die. (See

Mortality Table.) At age eighty, that would be $45,899. We will assume a 10 percent return on the initial $500,000 and the remainder each year thereafter, which amount will be added back into the estate.

If nothing is done to reduce the estate, other than the yearly-withdrawals on which to live, then the estate will grow each year to the point at which estate taxes will have to be paid. If the estate owner died after only five years, the heirs, after taxes, would receive $643,802; after ten years, $778,628; and after fifteen years (age eighty), $943,166. This takes into account only federal estate taxes, not legal fees or other administrative costs.

If one wished to give the $40,000 per year to heirs as the years passed and otherwise did exactly as above, the gifts would have to stop after ten years for the estate to last until age eighty. This passes on much less to heirs in the long run, even though it saves on estate taxes. With the same interest and inflation-rate assumptions, the heirs would get a total of $600,903 after five years if the estate owner died then; $586,670 after ten years; and only $433,631 after fifteen years (age eighty). Those figures take into account the $40,000 per year given during the first ten years. Also, if the person did live longer than age eighty, there would be nothing left but social security on which to live.

The plan proposed here would pass on $896,887 or $878,435 or $894,603 to heirs if the estate owner died after five, ten, or fifteen years respectively. The plan makes the same living requirement, inflation, and investment-return assumptions as both the above examples. It also assumes heirs who would be happy to cooperate in the plan. The following steps are necessary for the plan to work.

1. Purchase a $100,000 annuity which would pay $11,000+ (for a male at age sixty-five or $10,400 for a female) for each year for ten years or life, whichever is longer.
2. Purchase for the heirs insurance policies on the life of the estate owner which total $400,000 in death benefits. Each year the estate owner pays the premium on the policies (as part of each heir's $10,000 allowance). The heirs are both owners and beneficiaries of the policies. For a sixty-five-year-old male, $400,000 in cash-value life insurance can be purchased for $18,784 and $15,408 for a female aged sixty-five.
3. Each year the estate owner gives the difference between $40,000 and $18,784 to the heirs as cash gifts ($21,216). The figures above are based on a male age sixty-five. For a female, the amount passed on would be greater.
4. The heirs establish Clifford Trusts, with the estate owner as the beneficiary of the trusts. The heirs own the principal, but the estate owner receives the proceeds from investments, which he or she may apply to living requirements.
5. If the heirs wish, as the life insurance policies build up cash values, the money may be withdrawn for their use, since they are the owners. If so,

they must pay the interest on the loan (usually very low) and when the estate owner dies, the unrepaid loans will be deducted from the death benefit before paying the claims.

6. If the estate owner dies before the tenth year, the heirs also receive the annuity payments until ten years have passed.

A variation to this plan would be for the heirs to keep $8,000 per year instead of putting the whole $21,216 into the trusts. If they do that, the totals they would eventually receive after five, ten, or fifteen years would be $883,162, $817,942, and $734,712 respectively. If the estate owner just keeps the estate until he or she dies.

This plan or its variation gives the estate owner a comfortable living and passes on almost as much estate after many years (and much, much more if death occurs in the early years of the plan) than if the owner just keeps the estate until he or she dies. The heirs also have current use of at least some of the money.

Charitable Giving

Most churches have regional and/or national foundations which administer the investment assets of the churches' colleges, seminaries, orphanages, and so on. These organizations have plans which benefit both a giver of property and the receiving institution or mission program. Charitable giving can not only reduce the taxable estate of the giver but also be used by institutions to carry on a ministry the giver feels is worthwhile.

The best illustration of this is when a person has property, usually real estate or stocks or bonds, which was obtained many years ago and has appreciated greatly in value. If the property is left in the estate, the value will be eroded by estate taxes. If it is given to a charitable institution, several good things can happen. First, the estate value is decreased, eventually reducing estate taxes. Second, most charitable organizations can make agreements so that the income from the property goes to the giver until the giver and spouse die. The giver benefits as if he still owned the property, but at death the property is not taxed in his estate. Or a life annuity can be issued, in which the institution guarantees the giver a monthly income related to the value of the gift property, not to income from the property. This allows the institution to keep or sell the property at the most opportune time while still giving a monthly income to the giver.

There are many variations on the above idea and most foundations or institutions have a person on the staff to help you carry out your wishes. Contact them for more ideas, or write to me, and I will put you into contact with someone in your area.

Intra-Family Loans

Another way to pass on estate benefits before one's death is to make interest-free loans to children or other family members. This could be done

120

so children could buy a home or so that parents could let the children begin investing under supervision. One does not need a large estate for this plan.

If a person had $50,000 that he/she wished to leave to children, before his/her death, an interest-free loan could be made now. The child could do, for example, purchase a home with it. If the child had a down payment that left a balance due of $50,000, a 12 percent note would require monthly payments of $527 principal and interest for 25 years, for a total cost of $158,100. If a parent loaned a child the $50,000 to be paid back interest-free at $527 per month, it would save the child $108,100 and the parent would have the money back within eight years. The parent would have given up interest of the portion of the $50,000 unpaid each month, but the parent's interest loss is less than one-third what the child would save in interest. Thus the loan becomes an estate tool that can be used now with great benefit.

A proper contract needs to be drawn up for repayment so the IRS will not consider this a gift. One can even make the loan a payment-of-demand loan rather than one with monthly payments. If nothing is paid back within three years, the contract needs to be updated to keep IRS happy.

Checklist for Handling a Death in the Family

Immediately

_____ Call the doctor if not already in attendance. Follow his instructions.

_____ Call ambulance if death occurs at home.

_____ Call a trusted friend to help you (one who could come over immediately).

_____ Call pastor.

_____ Ask friend to call other friends and relatives. (Even if you wish to talk to them, let the friend do the calling.)

_____ Call funeral home and make preliminary arrangements.

_____ Think about
  ( ) Pallbearers. (If deceased was a member of an organization such as Rotary, Amerian Legion, you might ask them to furnish pallbearers and leave those arrangements to them.)

  ( ) Music.

  ( ) Burial plot.

  ( ) Burial date and time. (Allow time for those coming some distance to arrive, but do not delay past reasonable time.)

After the Funeral

_____ Talk with family financial advisor. (Do not make any major decisions such as selling the house, moving to a new town, until the initial shock of the death has passed.)

_____ Talk with attorney.

_____ Visit bank and inventory safe deposit box.

_____ Get insurance policies together and write or have someone else write to insurance companies. (Copies of death certificates will be needed and can be obtained from county clerk.)

_____ Contact creditors to see if debts are covered by insurance. (Most home mortgages, auto loans, and many smaller debts are covered, so that at the death of the head of household, debt is paid by creditor insurance.)

_____ Contact these persons or agencies as applicable:
  ( ) Social Security Administration
  ( ) Company or union representative in charge of benefits
  ( ) Veterans Administration

Record of Insurance and Other Important Data

Insurance: (A) Life, (B) Property, (C) Health, (D) Auto, (E) Other					
Person/Item Insured	Issuing Company	Policy Nmber	Face Value	Cash/Loan Value	Yearly Payments

Location of Important Documents

Wills:

Insurance policies:

Birth certificates:

Stock certificates:

Bank passbooks:

Other:

Contents of Safe Deposit Box(es) (List location)

Sample Situations and Strategies

Below are sample plans for young single persons as well as for several families with adults and children. My prejudice is that purely financial planning should generally be made around the chief breadwinner, whether male or female. However, since the point of this workbook is for you to devise a unique, personalized plan for your family, you may have different criteria than those in the samples. Adjust the illustrations to fit your circumstances.

Single Persons

While a single member of the clergy should go through the process of lifeline planning just as a married one, there are a few areas that are different for a single person. Because the single person has no one else on whom to rely in times of disaster or emergency (such as a spouse who would be able to work if a marriage partner becomes disabled), he or she needs to make careful provisions for such situations. First, there should be in effect a large savings program to cover such times, or a very good disability-income insurance, or a combination of both. Next, a very sound retirement plan must be worked out (see chapters on investments and retirement). Finally, there should be enough life insurance to pay any unpaid bills at one's death and provide for funeral expenses. While married persons may also have interests outside the family, the single person is probably in a better position to use life insurance to make contributions to groups, organizations, or activities in which he or she has great interest. A life insurance program such as a married person may have to insure the children's education could be used by a single person to endow a scholarship fund or just to make a large contribution to an organization or activity upon death. By using permanent-type policies, you can see the good of these contributions while still living (the organization can use the cash value even before you die)—and premium payments are then tax deductible. Speaking of taxes, single people often need more tax sheltering than married couples, so a good tax advisor should be consulted on ways to reduce tax obligations.

There are some singles who have responsibilities similar to those of married persons. Single persons may have aging parents or other relatives for whom they are financially responsible. Singles who are widowed or divorced may have children of varying ages just as a married couple, but since there is only one adult in the family, all the responsibility rests on that person. In those cases, the lifeline planning, insurance protection, and other programs will probably be very much like that of a married person, with the added provision that a single person has the sole responsibility.

There is one other consideration for young singles. Even those who do not expect to marry should make a few of the same tentative provisions (for a while) that are made by singles who do plan or hope to get married someday. A person who expects to be married might wish to do such things as travel before settling down. One ought to do some things while young, to benefit in the future from the experience and because the cost will probably never be any less. It is also a good idea to get at least a small permanent insurance policy with an option to purchase more life insurance in the future, regardless of health. Anyone might need more life insurance in the future, single or married. Both of those are good ideas for single persons who are young, whether or not they actually do get married.

Married, Age Forty

The hypothetical subject for the illustration in the text (see chapter 3), is a married male, age thirty, with a wife and two small children. But it matters not whether the clergy member of the family is male or female. My plan should work for either, so this illustration will assume the female as clergy and the husband as a schoolteacher. She is forty, her husband is forty-five, and they have two children age sixteen and eighteen. They have made a decision years before that since he can teach almost anywhere, they will move whenever she has a career opportunity, just as other clergy families do when the husband is the minister. Their major concern is seeing that their children get the same kind of education they had, at least college and perhaps graduate school. They have some savings but not enough to get the children through school.

Many people wait until their children get to college and then put together what they can and borrow the rest, paying it back years after the children have finished school. While that may be one way to handle things, an alternative would be to sit down earlier and try to work out with the children how much it is going to cost, involving them in the process. After deciding what one might need to borrow, go ahead and borrow that amount, invest it and start making the payments on the note. The cost of borrowing will be less that way—because the invested money will be earning interest and the actual cost will be only the difference between the earned interest and the interest on the note. If one waits until the time the money is needed, the cost will be the entire amount of the loan interest.

Otherwise, this couple would make use of lifeline planning just as the younger example, except that they have to figure in the repayment of the college debt (if they need to borrow for that). Retirement planning, insurance, and other aspects of their program would be very similar to the illustration in the text. A slight difference would occur in the insurance program. While a young person has time both to insure college costs for children and make investments toward that end, the older person only has time to insure and do a little investing. Thus a larger amount of insurance may be needed. Since it will be needed for a shorter time, purchase the least expensive annually renewable term available. Although decreasing-term policies may seem attractive because the need gets less each year the children get nearer to being finished, for a short period of time, annually renewable term is generally less expensive than decreasing term.

Married, Age Fifty

This example is for a married male, age fifty, who is married and whose children have been gone from home for a few years. The couple's main concern now is to be able to accomplish the goals on their lifeline (such as travel) and to plan well for retirement. This family should, just as the others, do the lifeline planning from their current ages to retirement and death. A suggestion for those in this situation would be to look at the cash-value life insurance they may have taken out years before. If they have not previously borrowed from the policies, or if they did and paid the loans back, there might be substantial money available to invest in higher-rate-of-return instruments (financial jargon for C.D.'s, stocks, and so on). The charts in Appendix F show that a person who has been using dividends to purchase paid-up additions on a cash-value permanent-life policy probably cannot do much better with the same money put into term insurance and the difference invested. However, if the dividends are not buying paid-up additions (or perhaps the policy does not even pay dividends), the cash value should be borrowed and invested. You must pay the insurance company the small interest rate guaranteed in the policy, but since you should be able to make much more on your investments, you will still come out ahead.

If you are not good with investments or just don't want to worry about them, call some insurance companies that sell the new universal-life policies which give the protection of life insurance and cash buildup based on either current interest rates of an instrument such as stocks. The only problem with these policies right now is the question of how money withdrawn in the future will be taxed. Since you generally have to pay taxes on investment earnings anyway, do not let that stop you. It might even be advantageous to trade in your older policies for the newer one.

Married, Age Sixty

If you have waited this long to begin planning for retirement, it will be difficult but not impossible. Anyone in this age group should do the lifeline planning just as younger persons do but the emphasis will probably be along a much different line. First, you should use the last few years of full-time work to invest and plan for retirement. If you do not own a place to live, that should probably also be a very high priority item, for that will be a big need in retirement. If you have a hospitalization plan that will last into retirement, fine; if not, one should definitely be taken out.

The next thing to do is take care of retirement income. Most pension plans, even with social security, will not let you live well, but only at a minimal comfort level. A private retirement plan should be started, if this is not already being done. The 403b tax-sheltered annuity plan mentioned in chapter 11 has some special provisions for adding more than the normally allowed amounts during the last few years before retirement. These provisions are called the year-of-separation-from-service limitation, the any-year limitations, and the overall limitations (IRS Code Section 415 (c) (4) A, B, and C). Ask your tax consultant about this or call your insurance agent.

If you are one of those fortunate few who have enough money not only to live well in retirement, but to create a potential estate problem, see Appendix K for a suggestion on how to handle it.

Monthly Budget Worksheet

Month of _____ *198* __

Budget Category	Yearly Budget	Monthly Budget	Spent this Month	Spent this Year
Church/Charities				
Savings/Investments				
Food/Household Items				
Clothing				
Housing: Mortgage/Rent				
Utilities				
Furniture/Miscellaneous				
Transportation: Auto Payments				
Gas, Oil, Etc.				
Insurance				
Repairs/Maintenance				
Miscellaneous				
Medical (doctor, dentist, medicine)				
Personal Taxes (income/other)				
Insurance (life, health, other)				
Allowances/Personal Care				
Entertainment (at home and away)				
Celebrations (holidays, birthdays, anniversaries, etc.)				
Rest/Relaxation (vacations, hobbies, recreation, etc.)				
Education/Enrichment (art/music lessons, books, etc.				
Professional Expenses (tools, books, schools, not paid by employer)				
Community Involvement (political parties, scouting, etc.)				
Prior Debt Retirement				
Miscellaneous				
TOTALS				

Monthly Expenditures
Month of _____, 19 __

On Account With And/Or Budget Category	Previous Balance	Add/Subtract Charges, Credits, Interest, etc.	Pay this Month	New Balance
Total				

Monthly Budget Worksheet
Month of _____ *198* __

Budget Category	Yearly Budget	Monthly Budget	Spent this Month	Spent this Year
Church/Charities				
Savings/Investments				
Food/Household Items				
Clothing				
Housing: Mortgage/Rent				
Utilities				
Furniture/Miscellaneous				
Transportation: Auto Payments				
Gas, Oil, Etc.				
Insurance				
Repairs/Maintenance				
Miscellaneous				
Medical (doctor, dentist, medicine)				
Personal Taxes (income/other)				
Insurance (life, health, other)				
Allowances/Personal Care				
Entertainment (at home and away)				
Celebrations (holidays, birthdays, anniversaries, etc.)				
Rest/Relaxation (vacations, hobbies, recreation, etc.)				
Education/Enrichment (art/music lessons, books, etc.				
Professional Expenses (tools, books, schools, not paid by employer)				
Community Involvement (political parties, scouting, etc.)				
Prior Debt Retirement				
Miscellaneous				
TOTALS				

Monthly Expenditures
Month of _____, 19 ___

On Account With And/Or Budget Category		Previous Balance	Add/Subtract Charges, Credits, Interest, etc.	Pay this Month	New Balance
Total					

Monthly Budget Worksheet
Month of _____ *198* __

Budget Category	Yearly Budget	Monthly Budget	Spent this Month	Spent this Year
Church/Charities				
Savings/Investments				
Food/Household Items				
Clothing				
Housing: Mortgage/Rent				
Utilities				
Furniture/Miscellaneous				
Transportation: Auto Payments				
Gas, Oil, Etc.				
Insurance				
Repairs/Maintenance				
Miscellaneous				
Medical (doctor, dentist, medicine)				
Personal Taxes (income/other)				
Insurance (life, health, other)				
Allowances/Personal Care				
Entertainment (at home and away)				
Celebrations (holidays, birthdays, anniversaries, etc.)				
Rest/Relaxation (vacations, hobbies, recreation, etc.)				
Education/Enrichment (art/music lessons, books, etc.				
Professional Expenses (tools, books, schools, not paid by employer)				
Community Involvement (political parties, scouting, etc.)				
Prior Debt Retirement				
Miscellaneous				
TOTALS				

Monthly Expenditures
Month of _____, 19 __

On Account With And/Or Budget Category	Previous Balance	Add/Subtract Charges, Credits, Interest, etc.	Pay this Month	New Balance
Total				

Monthly Budget Worksheet
Month of _____ *198* __

Budget Category	Yearly Budget	Monthly Budget	Spent this Month	Spent this Year
Church/Charities				
Savings/Investments				
Food/Household Items				
Clothing				
Housing: Mortgage/Rent				
Utilities				
Furniture/Miscellaneous				
Transportation: Auto Payments				
Gas, Oil, Etc.				
Insurance				
Repairs/Maintenance				
Miscellaneous				
Medical (doctor, dentist, medicine)				
Personal Taxes (income/other)				
Insurance (life, health, other)				
Allowances/Personal Care				
Entertainment (at home and away)				
Celebrations (holidays, birthdays, anniversaries, etc.)				
Rest/Relaxation (vacations, hobbies, recreation, etc.)				
Education/Enrichment (art/music lessons, books, etc.				
Professional Expenses (tools, books, schools, not paid by employer)				
Community Involvement (political parties, scouting, etc.)				
Prior Debt Retirement				
Miscellaneous				
TOTALS				

Monthly Expenditures
Month of _____, *19* ___

On Account With And/Or Budget Category		Previous Balance	Add/Subtract Charges, Credits, Interest, etc.	Pay this Month	New Balance
Total					

Monthly Budget Worksheet

Month of _____ *198* __

Budget Category	Yearly Budget	Monthly Budget	Spent this Month	Spent this Year
Church/Charities				
Savings/Investments				
Food/Household Items				
Clothing				
Housing: Mortgage/Rent				
Utilities				
Furniture/Miscellaneous				
Transportation: Auto Payments				
Gas, Oil, Etc.				
Insurance				
Repairs/Maintenance				
Miscellaneous				
Medical (doctor, dentist, medicine)				
Personal Taxes (income/other)				
Insurance (life, health, other)				
Allowances/Personal Care				
Entertainment (at home and away)				
Celebrations (holidays, birthdays, anniversaries, etc.)				
Rest/Relaxation (vacations, hobbies, recreation, etc.)				
Education/Enrichment (art/music lessons, books, etc.				
Professional Expenses (tools, books, schools, not paid by employer)				
Community Involvement (political parties, scouting, etc.)				
Prior Debt Retirement				
Miscellaneous				
TOTALS				

Monthly Expenditures
Month of _____, *19* __

On Account With And/Or Budget Category		Previous Balance	Add/Subtract Charges, Credits, Interest, etc.	Pay this Month	New Balance
Total					

Monthly Budget Worksheet
Month of _____ *198* __

Budget Category	Yearly Budget	Monthly Budget	Spent this Month	Spent this Year
Church/Charities				
Savings/Investments				
Food/Household Items				
Clothing				
Housing: Mortgage/Rent				
Utilities				
Furniture/Miscellaneous				
Transportation: Auto Payments				
Gas, Oil, Etc.				
Insurance				
Repairs/Maintenance				
Miscellaneous				
Medical (doctor, dentist, medicine)				
Personal Taxes (income/other)				
Insurance (life, health, other)				
Allowances/Personal Care				
Entertainment (at home and away)				
Celebrations (holidays, birthdays, anniversaries, etc.)				
Rest/Relaxation (vacations, hobbies, recreation, etc.)				
Education/Enrichment (art/music lessons, books, etc.				
Professional Expenses (tools, books, schools, not paid by employer)				
Community Involvement (political parties, scouting, etc.)				
Prior Debt Retirement				
Miscellaneous				
TOTALS				

Monthly Expenditures
Month of _____, 19 __

On Account With And/Or Budget Category	Previous Balance	Add/Subtract Charges, Credits, Interest, etc.	Pay this Month	New Balance
Total				

Monthly Budget Worksheet
Month of _____ 198 __

Budget Category	Yearly Budget	Monthly Budget	Spent this Month	Spent this Year
Church/Charities				
Savings/Investments				
Food/Household Items				
Clothing				
Housing: Mortgage/Rent				
Utilities				
Furniture/Miscellaneous				
Transportation: Auto Payments				
Gas, Oil, Etc.				
Insurance				
Repairs/Maintenance				
Miscellaneous				
Medical (doctor, dentist, medicine)				
Personal Taxes (income/other)				
Insurance (life, health, other)				
Allowances/Personal Care				
Entertainment (at home and away)				
Celebrations (holidays, birthdays, anniversaries, etc.)				
Rest/Relaxation (vacations, hobbies, recreation, etc.)				
Education/Enrichment (art/music lessons, books, etc.				
Professional Expenses (tools, books, schools, not paid by employer)				
Community Involvement (political parties, scouting, etc.)				
Prior Debt Retirement				
Miscellaneous				
TOTALS				

Monthly Expenditures
Month of _____, 19 __

On Account With And/Or Budget Category		Previous Balance	Add/Subtract Charges, Credits, Interest, etc.	Pay this Month	New Balance
Total					

Monthly Budget Worksheet
Month of _____ 198 __

Budget Category	Yearly Budget	Monthly Budget	Spent this Month	Spent this Year
Church/Charities				
Savings/Investments				
Food/Household Items				
Clothing				
Housing: Mortgage/Rent				
Utilities				
Furniture/Miscellaneous				
Transportation: Auto Payments				
Gas, Oil, Etc.				
Insurance				
Repairs/Maintenance				
Miscellaneous				
Medical (doctor, dentist, medicine)				
Personal Taxes (income/other)				
Insurance (life, health, other)				
Allowances/Personal Care				
Entertainment (at home and away)				
Celebrations (holidays, birthdays, anniversaries, etc.)				
Rest/Relaxation (vacations, hobbies, recreation, etc.)				
Education/Enrichment (art/music lessons, books, etc.				
Professional Expenses (tools, books, schools, not paid by employer)				
Community Involvement (political parties, scouting, etc.)				
Prior Debt Retirement				
Miscellaneous				
TOTALS				

Monthly Expenditures
Month of _____, 19 __

On Account With And/Or Budget Category		Previous Balance	Add/Subtract Charges, Credits, Interest, etc.	Pay this Month	New Balance
Total					

Monthly Budget Worksheet
Month of _____ 198 __

Budget Category	Yearly Budget	Monthly Budget	Spent this Month	Spent this Year
Church/Charities				
Savings/Investments				
Food/Household Items				
Clothing				
Housing: Mortgage/Rent				
Utilities				
Furniture/Miscellaneous				
Transportation: Auto Payments				
Gas, Oil, Etc.				
Insurance				
Repairs/Maintenance				
Miscellaneous				
Medical (doctor, dentist, medicine)				
Personal Taxes (income/other)				
Insurance (life, health, other)				
Allowances/Personal Care				
Entertainment (at home and away)				
Celebrations (holidays, birthdays, anniversaries, etc.)				
Rest/Relaxation (vacations, hobbies, recreation, etc.)				
Education/Enrichment (art/music lessons, books, etc.				
Professional Expenses (tools, books, schools, not paid by employer)				
Community Involvement (political parties, scouting, etc.)				
Prior Debt Retirement				
Miscellaneous				
TOTALS				

Monthly Expenditures
Month of _____, 19 __

On Account With And/Or Budget Category		Previous Balance	Add/Subtract Charges, Credits, Interest, etc.	Pay this Month	New Balance
Total					

Monthly Budget Worksheet

Month of _____ *198* __

Budget Category	Yearly Budget	Monthly Budget	Spent this Month	Spent this Year
Church/Charities				
Savings/Investments				
Food/Household Items				
Clothing				
Housing: Mortgage/Rent				
Utilities				
Furniture/Miscellaneous				
Transportation: Auto Payments				
Gas, Oil, Etc.				
Insurance				
Repairs/Maintenance				
Miscellaneous				
Medical (doctor, dentist, medicine)				
Personal Taxes (income/other)				
Insurance (life, health, other)				
Allowances/Personal Care				
Entertainment (at home and away)				
Celebrations (holidays, birthdays, anniversaries, etc.)				
Rest/Relaxation (vacations, hobbies, recreation, etc.)				
Education/Enrichment (art/music lessons, books, etc.				
Professional Expenses (tools, books, schools, not paid by employer)				
Community Involvement (political parties, scouting, etc.)				
Prior Debt Retirement				
Miscellaneous				
TOTALS				

Monthly Expenditures
Month of _____, 19 __

On Account With And/Or Budget Category	Previous Balance	Add/Subtract Charges, Credits, Interest, etc.	Pay this Month	New Balance
Total				

Monthly Budget Worksheet
Month of _____ *198* __

Budget Category	Yearly Budget	Monthly Budget	Spent this Month	Spent this Year
Church/Charities				
Savings/Investments				
Food/Household Items				
Clothing				
Housing: Mortgage/Rent				
Utilities				
Furniture/Miscellaneous				
Transportation: Auto Payments				
Gas, Oil, Etc.				
Insurance				
Repairs/Maintenance				
Miscellaneous				
Medical (doctor, dentist, medicine)				
Personal Taxes (income/other)				
Insurance (life, health, other)				
Allowances/Personal Care				
Entertainment (at home and away)				
Celebrations (holidays, birthdays, anniversaries, etc.)				
Rest/Relaxation (vacations, hobbies, recreation, etc.)				
Education/Enrichment (art/music lessons, books, etc.				
Professional Expenses (tools, books, schools, not paid by employer)				
Community Involvement (political parties, scouting, etc.)				
Prior Debt Retirement				
Miscellaneous				
TOTALS				

Monthly Expenditures
Month of ＿＿＿＿＿, 19 ＿

On Account With And/Or Budget Category	Previous Balance	Add/Subtract Charges, Credits, Interest, etc.	Pay this Month	New Balance
Total				

Monthly Budget Worksheet

Month of _____ *198* __

Budget Category	Yearly Budget	Monthly Budget	Spent this Month	Spent this Year
Church/Charities				
Savings/Investments				
Food/Household Items				
Clothing				
Housing: Mortgage/Rent				
Utilities				
Furniture/Miscellaneous				
Transportation: Auto Payments				
Gas, Oil, Etc.				
Insurance				
Repairs/Maintenance				
Miscellaneous				
Medical (doctor, dentist, medicine)				
Personal Taxes (income/other)				
Insurance (life, health, other)				
Allowances/Personal Care				
Entertainment (at home and away)				
Celebrations (holidays, birthdays, anniversaries, etc.)				
Rest/Relaxation (vacations, hobbies, recreation, etc.)				
Education/Enrichment (art/music lessons, books, etc.				
Professional Expenses (tools, books, schools, not paid by employer)				
Community Involvement (political parties, scouting, etc.)				
Prior Debt Retirement				
Miscellaneous				
TOTALS				

Monthly Expenditures
Month of _____, 19 __

On Account With And/Or Budget Category		Previous Balance	Add/Subtract Charges, Credits, Interest, etc.	Pay this Month	New Balance
Total					

Monthly Budget Worksheet
Month of _____ *198* __

Budget Category	Yearly Budget	Monthly Budget	Spent this Month	Spent this Year
Church/Charities				
Savings/Investments				
Food/Household Items				
Clothing				
Housing: Mortgage/Rent				
Utilities				
Furniture/Miscellaneous				
Transportation: Auto Payments				
Gas, Oil, Etc.				
Insurance				
Repairs/Maintenance				
Miscellaneous				
Medical (doctor, dentist, medicine)				
Personal Taxes (income/other)				
Insurance (life, health, other)				
Allowances/Personal Care				
Entertainment (at home and away)				
Celebrations (holidays, birthdays, anniversaries, etc.)				
Rest/Relaxation (vacations, hobbies, recreation, etc.)				
Education/Enrichment (art/music lessons, books, etc.				
Professional Expenses (tools, books, schools, not paid by employer)				
Community Involvement (political parties, scouting, etc.)				
Prior Debt Retirement				
Miscellaneous				
TOTALS				

Monthly Expenditures
Month of ———————, *19* —

On Account With And/Or Budget Category		Previous Balance	Add/Subtract Charges, Credits, Interest, etc.	Pay this Month	New Balance
Total					

Monthly Budget Worksheet

Month of _____ *198* __

Budget Category	Yearly Budget	Monthly Budget	Spent this Month	Spent this Year
Church/Charities				
Savings/Investments				
Food/Household Items				
Clothing				
Housing: Mortgage/Rent				
Utilities				
Furniture/Miscellaneous				
Transportation: Auto Payments				
Gas, Oil, Etc.				
Insurance				
Repairs/Maintenance				
Miscellaneous				
Medical (doctor, dentist, medicine)				
Personal Taxes (income/other)				
Insurance (life, health, other)				
Allowances/Personal Care				
Entertainment (at home and away)				
Celebrations (holidays, birthdays, anniversaries, etc.)				
Rest/Relaxation (vacations, hobbies, recreation, etc.)				
Education/Enrichment (art/music lessons, books, etc.				
Professional Expenses (tools, books, schools, not paid by employer)				
Community Involvement (political parties, scouting, etc.)				
Prior Debt Retirement				
Miscellaneous				
TOTALS				

Monthly Expenditures
Month of _____, 19 __

On Account With And/Or Budget Category	Previous Balance	Add/Subtract Charges, Credits, Interest, etc.	Pay this Month	New Balance
Total				

Monthly Budget Worksheet

Month of _____ 198 __

Budget Category	Yearly Budget	Monthly Budget	Spent this Month	Spent this Year
Church/Charities				
Savings/Investments				
Food/Household Items				
Clothing				
Housing: Mortgage/Rent				
Utilities				
Furniture/Miscellaneous				
Transportation: Auto Payments				
Gas, Oil, Etc.				
Insurance				
Repairs/Maintenance				
Miscellaneous				
Medical (doctor, dentist, medicine)				
Personal Taxes (income/other)				
Insurance (life, health, other)				
Allowances/Personal Care				
Entertainment (at home and away)				
Celebrations (holidays, birthdays, anniversaries, etc.)				
Rest/Relaxation (vacations, hobbies, recreation, etc.)				
Education/Enrichment (art/music lessons, books, etc.				
Professional Expenses (tools, books, schools, not paid by employer)				
Community Involvement (political parties, scouting, etc.)				
Prior Debt Retirement				
Miscellaneous				
TOTALS				

Monthly Expenditures
Month of _____, 19 __

On Account With And/Or Budget Category		Previous Balance	Add/Subtract Charges, Credits, Interest, etc.	Pay this Month	New Balance
Total					

Monthly Budget Worksheet

Month of _____ *198* __

Budget Category	Yearly Budget	Monthly Budget	Spent this Month	Spent this Year
Church/Charities				
Savings/Investments				
Food/Household Items				
Clothing				
Housing: Mortgage/Rent				
Utilities				
Furniture/Miscellaneous				
Transportation: Auto Payments				
Gas, Oil, Etc.				
Insurance				
Repairs/Maintenance				
Miscellaneous				
Medical (doctor, dentist, medicine)				
Personal Taxes (income/other)				
Insurance (life, health, other)				
Allowances/Personal Care				
Entertainment (at home and away)				
Celebrations (holidays, birthdays, anniversaries, etc.)				
Rest/Relaxation (vacations, hobbies, recreation, etc.)				
Education/Enrichment (art/music lessons, books, etc.				
Professional Expenses (tools, books, schools, not paid by employer)				
Community Involvement (political parties, scouting, etc.)				
Prior Debt Retirement				
Miscellaneous				
TOTALS				

Monthly Expenditures
Month of _____, 19 __

On Account With And/Or Budget Category		Previous Balance	Add/Subtract Charges, Credits, Interest, etc.	Pay this Month	New Balance
Total					